41 Shades of Grey
The Tweet Life
of Stoke City

41 Shades... is David Lee's 12th book, and his 5th about Stoke City. Other Stokie books include You Could'ner Make It Up! and Stoke City's Greatest Games.

He has also written a best-selling biography of Tony Pulis entitled Triffic!, and a 50th anniversary book on England's World Cup winners, The Golden Boys Of '66.

His irreverent humour is often seen oozing gamely out of a number of 'papers and periodicals. Naturally enough he's a Twitter man.

41 Shades of Grey
The Tweet Life
of Stoke City

Edited by **David Lee**

DB
PUBLISHING

First Publishied in Great Britain in 2017 by DB Publishing,
an imprint of JMD Media Ltd

ISBN 978-1-78091-557-9

Printed and bound in the UK

Terry Conroy @TerryConroy

Good luck with trying to make 2016/17 season better than it was.

Acknowledgments

Thank you to all the Tweeters for allowing us to reproduce their work. For this reason we applaud their ability to capture the emotion of the moment, but we hope no one is offended by what can often be just raw emotion. We have tried to faithfully and accurately reproduce the Tweets – warts, typos and all – but if there are discrepancies, we apologise and simply blame the technology! Enjoy.

Introduction

Well, what a memorable season it's been for Stoke City!

- An inspired start that had all the experts reaching for their record books!
- Performances that had supporters jumping up and down excitedly in their seats!
- That fabled cup run, only tragically ended at home to a half-strength lowly Championship side!
- A historic 100th Premier goal celebration by Peter Crouch!
- And of course, silverware! The Staffordshire Senior Cup, won against all the odds against high-flying Chasetown…on penalties!

Er, yeah, it doesn't sound quite so impressive now I've found it on a scrap of paper that I scribbled on down the pub.

But what is memorable about last season was the high standard of Stoke City tweets that fans shared with the world on Twitter.

Bold, personal, heart-warming, blistering, insightful, poignant, refreshing; yes, all great words, but probably not very relevant here, I'm afraid. No.

You see, this book is a collection of Tweets by a selection of Stokie Tweeters, whose views have coloured-in what many might feel was a dull black-and-white season. And thus, very much like a colour TV licence, we can charge more for it.

So sit back, stand up straight, find your reading-glasses, put the cat out, get a cup of tea, and then go back into the lounge and try and remember what you came in the room for.

You are here to re-live Stoke's 2016-17 season through the eyes of some excitable Stokies, who may not have enjoyed every moment, but certainly make it sound like the most wonderful experience. If you weren't there, you'll wish you had been.

Ah, you just can't write stuff like this. But these guys are having a brave attempt.

01/07/2016   Pre-season…

(As the traditionally disappointing summer of the Euros - can anyone actually remember Portugal winning it? - drifts away into the distance, Stoke City Tweeters slowly wake from their summer slumber. They yawn, stretch and look around, and feel happy and contented… for about 5 minutes. Then the caffeine and the adrenaline begin to kick in. Meanwhile, at the newly named bet365 stadium (anyone caught calling it "The Brit" will be roughly evicted), the wheels are being put back on the Stoke City wagon after a weak ending to the previous season. Joe Allen and Ramadan Sobhi are signed in July… Stoke lose some pre-season games such as 0-3 at Burton (16th July)…Marco Arnautovic is being chased by Everton…Stoke to enter a side into the Checkatrade Trophy…and the continuous saga of Saido Berahino transfer from WBA rolls on…and on…)

28/06/2016
Dorset potter@cain_rosscain

Ref: Stoke transfers, have we actually signed ANYONE yet ?

01/07/2016
Dorset potter@cain_rosscain

What are we up to Bournemouth, Watford and Palace all getting stuck into the market and we are monitoring some players 😠 😠

02/07/2016
Dorset potter@cain_rosscain

The bad news is we haven't sighed anyone the good news is we are going to be one of the richest sides in the championship 😨

02/07/2016
Dorset potter@cain_rosscain

I hope Stoke are not putting all their eggs in one basket with Berahino still think it might go pear shaped 😥

08/07/2016
Espleypotter@Marcespley

Why does Imbula get grief for wearing gloves, for all we know he could have Raynauds

16/07/2016
Rob Doolan@ChiefDelilah

So, this 3-5-2 then eh?

16/07/2016
Danny Bowers@dannybowers10

Minority blowing a friendly out of proportion, good run out, nice to see the youngsters. Highlights we need a winger, cb,keeper and striker.

20/07/2016
Rob Doolan@ChiefDelilah

Allen, Sobhi, Berahino and a centre half (or two) would constitute a very tidy window for Stoke.

20/07/2016
Espleypotter@Marcespley

Joe Allen would be an incredible signing. Perfect eventual replacement for Whelan, or play with if we go 3-5-2

20/07/2016
David Cowlishaw@davidcowlishaw

Joe Allen, the best Welsh midfielder ever, beard frozen in the Stoke winds, feeding Shaqiri through balls like he was born to do it.

23/07/2016
Will@IamWillSCFC

If Joe Allen meets with Mark Hughes, he's a Stoke player, simple as. Hughes is excellent at selling the club and his vision.

25/07/2016
The Oatcake Fanzine@oatcakescfc

The New Messi - Y, The Alpine Messi - Y, The Egyptian Messi - Y, The Welsh Xavi - Y. #Stokelona

25/07/2016
Will@IamWillSCFC

Can't wait for the signing of the Welsh Whitehead to be announced. Instant hero status awaits in the Potteries

25/07/2016
Will@IamWillSCFC

If Stoke are only announcing one signing today then Sobhi it…

25/07/2016
Espleypotter@Marcespley

Don't know what's more embarrassing, thinking Allen would go back Swansea, or actually being a Swansea fan

26/07/2016
Dorset potter@cain_rosscain

Just need a knuckle draging cente back and Berahino or someone similar . And we're done . Ps try Amazon always works for me 😆😆

27/07/2016
DUCK MAGAZINE@DUCKmagstoke

So we're a club that can now fight off the likes of Everton to keep our best players and buy quality to add to the team, too?!?! WATTBA

27/07/2016
Dorset potter@cain_rosscain

Apologies Stoke for whingeing about this transfer window now go get us a striker 👏👏👏👏👏👏

27/07/2016
Will@IamWillSCFC

I'm amazed at this. Last Summer we couldn't keep N'Zonzi, this Summer we keep Arnautovic. Huge sign of what's happening at Stoke

27/07/2016
Will@IamWillSCFC

4 more years to finally come up with a song for Marko Arnautovic

28/07/2016
Espleypotter@Marcespley

Oh my what an eventful week, Stoke signing players and Everton fans trying to make excuses why Stoke keep signing their targets

01/08/2016
David Cowlishaw@davidcowlishaw

Take me back to Pulis days where nobody went away games because it was so horrible. Easy to get tickets then.

05/08/2016
David Lee@stoke_city_pub

Repeat after me: "We will NOT be snobby about this competition. We will NOT be snobby about this tinpot competition" #CheckatradeTrophy

05/08/2016
Martin Smith@SolarSmudge

Great night to be in Hannover as they win their first game of the season 4-0 at Kaiserslautern! Stoke v H3amburg tomorrow!!!

09/08/2016
Will@IamWillSCFC

we waste so many games waiting to sign players and then getting them fit/on the same wave length, it boils my piss

10/08/2016
Espleypotter@Marcespley

Yesterday ManCity were believed to be letting Bony go for £13mill. Next day Arsenal want to bid £30mill. Is Wenger a tool or what

10/08/2016
Will@IamWillSCFC

Are we seriously about to enter a new season with fuck all done to that back four and fuck all new up top?!

12/08/2016
Trouserdog@TrouserdogSCFC

Not religious but you'd hope sorting @JackButland_One's ankle would be top of God's 'To Do' list given the amount of prayers he's just heard

13/08/2016
Trouserdog@TrouserdogSCFC

10th STOKE: We need a CB and a decent back up keeper. Could be higher if we can add one or two players. #Prempredictions

13/08/16   Middlesbrough (1) 1 Stoke City (0) 1

(Brilliant curling free-kick equaliser by Xherdan Shaqiri makes everything alright as Stoke start slowly against newly promoted Boro. Joe Allen (£13m) comes on late to make debut. A 1-1 draw: Yes, it's Stoke's best ever start to a season under Mark Hughes!)

Premier League position: 8th=

Order on MotD: 6th out of 7. (Gary Lineker appears in underwear)

13/08/2016
Trouserdog@TrouserdogSCFC

If I was Sparky I wouldn't have done a HT team talk, I'd have just kicked every single one of them in the bollocks. He probably did.

13/08/2016
The Oatcake Fanzine@oatcakescfc

A poor half from Stoke. No threat up front and extremely suspect at the back. Both concerns we ended last season with in fact. #SCFC

13/08/2016
Rob Doolan@ChiefDelilah

Feel sorry for Diouf. Repeatedly ignored when in good positions.

13/08/2016
David Cowlishaw@davidcowlishaw

Convinced Giannelli Imbula might be the best player of all time.

13/08/2016
Trouserdog@TrouserdogSCFC

First half was about as much fun as staring into the bowl of an unflushed public toilet for 45 mins. Second half much better.

13/08/2016
Will@IamWillSCFC

Everyone still feeling super confident about our back four now? Was I still over reacting when I questioned not strengthening?

13/08/2016
David Cowlishaw@davidcowlishaw

Oh mate, when Shaq scored that goal. Limbs AOTS. #FootballsBack

13/08/2016
David Lee@stoke_city_pub

Stoke's first (direct) free-kick goal in Prem since October 2013!?!

13/08/2016
Rob Doolan@ChiefDelilah

The number three peeling away to the near post is a classic TP set piece move. Don't miss much about those days, but I miss that.

13/08/2016
Neil Finney@NeilFinney

enjoyable away day, we improved as the game developed. Impressive stadium, friendly locals. A decent point. #scfc

13/08/2016
Chris Ault@Chrisa020985

Gonna be strange picturing Shaqiri when I'm making love to the Mrs later but that's a pretty decent point away from home!

13/08/2016
Will@IamWillSCFC

pre-Injury, Jack was making more saves than any other keeper. Warning signs were there, but we just praised Jack instead

13/08/2016
David Lee@stoke_city_pub

Captain Birdseye (#Sparky) late back from catching fresh cod for team's fish fingers, reckons Glen Johnson's pulled a muscle below his bum! #pressconference

13/08/2016
Dave@davematthews79

Enjoyable awayday in @Boro. Decent ground and sound fans, hope they do well this season. Draw probably a fair result

13/08/2016
HAIRY POTTER@cosnakickbo

Middlesbrough 1 Stoke City 1 Potential #BananaSkin Dealt With 🍵🍺👍 #Shaqiri We are Off and Running

13/08/2016
David Cowlishaw@davidcowlishaw

Woah, possibly the worst MOTD titles in a while.

13/08/2016
Rob Doolan@ChiefDelilah

The greatest trick the devil ever pulled was making you actually eager to see a man present a football show in his underwear.

14/08/2016
The Oatcake Fanzine@oatcakescfc

Well there's a shock... First weekend of the season and #WengerOut is trending!

14/08/2016
Dorset potter@cain_rosscain

Think we are 8th that will do end the season now

20/08/16   Stoke City (0) 1 Manchester City (2) 4

(Is it a bird? Is it a plane?! Well, it certainly isn't a penalty, but that's ref Mike Dean for you. He's clearly been told to stop Stoke "grappling" in the box, so Stoke are 0-2 down by half-time. After missing a stonewall penalty on Joe Allen, he then gives Stoke the softest penalty ever to make amends, converted by Bojan Krkic. But it's downhill from there…)

Premier League position: 17th

Order on MotD: 2nd out of 8

20/08/2016
Neil Finney@NeilFinney

Windy and raining for Stokes first home game of the season. Perfect 😃#SCFC

20/08/2016
David Cowlishaw@davidcowlishaw

Diouf having a shocker. Bojan not a winger. Ref has fucked it. Discipline gone and they're comfortable. Apart from that all okay.

20/08/2016
Rob Doolan@ChiefDelilah

Whelan the man tasked with marking Aguero? Ok then...

20/08/2016
Trouserdog@TrouserdogSCFC

Joe Allen was like an angry little wasp buzzing everywhere in midfield. Unfortunately, next to him, Imbula was more like a dozy bumblebee.

20/08/2016
Rob Doolan@ChiefDelilah

At his worst, Imbula is that kid in the playground who thought he was too good to pass to anyone.

20/08/2016
Trouserdog@TrouserdogSCFC

If Man City are on their A-game and the ref has a boner for them then there's only going to be one result, sadly.

20/08/2016
Rob Doolan@ChiefDelilah

You never learn, do you Ryan?

20/08/2016
Will@IamWillSCFC

Do Shawcross and Wollscheid actually know each other? Do they speak? Because their partnership and understanding of each other is awful

20/08/2016
Rob Doolan@ChiefDelilah

So is that Diouf wide right or Bojan?

20/08/2016
Rob Doolan@ChiefDelilah

Bojan on the right is four different shades of screaming mental.

20/08/2016
Neil Finney@NeilFinney

we did OK in spells, 3 dodgy penalty calls. 2 late goals flattered them. I thought we'd pinch a draw at 2-1 #scfc

20/08/2016
Will@IamWillSCFC

it's a shame because I do like Hughes. Can't escape how bad we are though, it must change

20/08/2016
DUCK MAGAZINE@DUCKmagstoke

There's no big club bias. Just a coincidence that Allen gets floored and Costa gets 2 winners in games he shouldn't have been on the pitch.

20/08/2016
Will@IamWillSCFC

Can't accept that we were just beaten by a better team. We were a shambles at the back again and created absolutely nothing.

20/08/2016
David Lee@stoke_city_pub

Marc Wilson claimed #scfc not working hard enough in training on defence. Man City's goals reveal some truth in that. #stoke #SCFCvMCFC

20/08/2016
Dave@davematthews79

Didn't deserve to lose by such a margin, but we are toothless in attack and dodgy in defence. Joe Allen superb however!

21/08/2016
Terry Conroy@TerryConroy

Chairmans Suite very very quiet yesterday..No buzz, no heckling,no matchday former player either.!!

20/08/2016
Dave@davematthews79

New season but same old shit from Mike 'look at me' Dean. How this absolute knobhead is still refereeing is beyond me.

20/08/2016
Espleypotter@Marcespley

Stoke lose and we on second on MOTD

20/08/2016
DUCK MAGAZINE@DUCKmagstoke

Pep says our noise today was superb? Either my ears have gone or he's very patronising.

20/08/2016
Espleypotter@Marcespley

Imbula was poor today, we were over ran in midfield at times. Good job for Allen, Imbula only completed 11 passes all game

20/08/2016
Martin Smith@SolarSmudge

Well that was never a 4-1 game but that's what happens against good teams. Our defence is a major concern #scfc #mcfc

20/08/2016
Espleypotter@Marcespley

I truly hope Mike deans shits hedgehogs for the rest of his life. Most incompetent ref around

20/08/2016
Dorset potter@cain_rosscain

We will forgive letting 4 goals to Man City but if we can't compete with the top 5 we have to dominate the rest or we are going backwards

22/08/2016
HAIRY POTTER@cosnakickbo

Don't panic! "What Points Total Did You Expect after Playing Middlesbrough Away & Man City Home??? 11% - 6 or 4 Points, 30% - 3 Points, 21% - 2 Points, 38% - 1 or 0 Points"

23/08/16   Stevenage (0) 0 Stoke City (2) 4

(Peter Crouch scores a hat-trick, including a dangerous looking overhead scissor-kick, but full-back Phil Bardsley steals the show with left-footed rocket from several streets away. Harmless EFL cup fun…)

23/08/2016
StevenageFC Official @StevenageFC

Work in Stevenage? Why spend lunch at your desk when you can come and buy Luton & Stoke tickets PLUS get your car washed for £3.50? Bargain!

23/08/2016
David Cowlishaw@davidcowlishaw

No other young players bar Bachmann in the squad not only a shame but puts even more pressure on us to get a convincing result.

23/08/2016
Rob Doolan@ChiefDelilah

So we're definitely still calling it the 'EFL Cup' then? We've still decided that was a good idea?

23/08/2016
Dave@davematthews79

Since when have we started calling the League Cup the EFL Cup? Sounds very Americanized. The Rumbelows Cup sounded far more British!

23/08/2016
StevenageFC Official @StevenageFC

TIP: Home fans in the terraces might like to bring sunglasses tonight to avoid the evening sunshine blinding you! 😎

23/08/2016

Espleypotter@Marcespley

It's all good bringing young into the side, but you need to progress foremost. Pulis may have played a 16 year old but they got knocked out

23/08/2016
StevenageFC Official @StevenageFC

Who needs a cold, wet & windy night in Stoke when you have a gloriously hot & sunny day in Stevenage?

23/08/2016
Espleypotter@Marcespley

Bardsley hit that shot harder than he hit Wayne Rooney

23/08/2016
DUCK MAGAZINE@DUCKmagstoke

Can we not just be happy we're 4-0 up, no matter who the opposition?

23/08/2016
StevenageFC Official @StevenageFC

Safe journey home to all you @stokecity fans. Thanks for making the trip south and best of luck in the #EFLCup & Premier League this season.

24/08/2016
Martin Smith@SolarSmudge

Likely #EFLCup draw tonight... Chelsea v Northampton. Man Utd v Gillingham. Arsenal v Preston. World XI v Stoke City. #rigged #bigclubs

27/08/16   Everton (0) 1 Stoke City (0) 0

(England manager, Sam Allardyce, looks on in disbelief as Shay Given saves a dodgy penalty, only for the ball to hit the post, bounce off the back of his head and into the goal. You Could'ner Make It Up! Big Sam lasts another 31 days, Shay only 22)

Premier League position: 20th

Order on MotD: 6th out of 8

27/08/2016
Will@IamWillSCFC

Could pay a fortune to head up the motorway to Everton, get treated like shit by police, covered in beer and have the top taken off my coke

---

27/08/2016
Will@IamWillSCFC

Doesn't take anything away from my love of Stoke. You just don't realise how far away from football the current PL away day experience is

---

27/08/2016
Trouserdog@TrouserdogSCFC

Hughes has 4 midfielders (Afellay, Adam, Imbula and Allen) vying for the same midfield spot if we play 4-2-3-1. Terrible squad management

---

27/08/2016
DUCK MAGAZINE@DUCKmagstoke

He may not be ready, but surely Sobhi, a wide player, is a far better bet than putting Dioufy out there. Feel sorry for the bloke

27/08/2016
Trouserdog@TrouserdogSCFC

Crouch looked lonely up-front, Imbula looked lazy in midfield, Diouf (as always) looked hopeless on the wing. Sort it out MH

27/08/2016
HAIRY POTTER@cosnakickbo

Big Sams had Enough !!! EVEvSTO

27/08/2016
Neil Finney@NeilFinney

A few of our players in a hurry to get off the pitch at the end. Cheers lads.

27/08/2016
David Cowlishaw@davidcowlishaw

Deservedly lost. Mark Hughes still doesn't know what his best team is. An improved defensive performance the big positive.

27/08/2016
The Oatcake Fanzine@oatcakescfc

Got to feel for Michael Oliver today. Wins a penalty single-handedly and Leighton Baines won't let him take it. #EVESTO

27/08/2016
Terry Conroy@TerryConroy

Enjoyed my return summarising for BBC Radio Stoke.Didn't enjoy Referees performanceWe played well against a good side need the breaks though

27/08/2016
David Cowlishaw@davidcowlishaw

Some classic Stokefanitis today. Nobody moaned at Allen for his sloppy passes but Imbula got pelters whenever he lost possession.

27/08/2016
Will@IamWillSCFC

Wollscheid is back in Germany with an ear problem. His right one is probably on fire with the amount of shite talked about him on here

28/08/2016
Terry Conroy@TerryConroy

Surely the Premier League Referees Management body are aware of the inconsistencies of the Matchday Officials.What will they do about it?

28/08/2016
Terry Conroy@TerryConroy

As usual,they will do nothing.!Two games highlighted the ineptness of the Ref.Spurs v LPool,Leicester v Swansea.Huthy nearly mauled to death

28/08/2016
David Cowlishaw@davidcowlishaw

Seen myself on Match of the Day. Woohoo.

(After seemingly criticising Stoke's defensive training methods, Marc Wilson (wildog87) leaves to join Bournemouth then later WBA…Wollscheid never plays for Stoke again, & is loaned out to Wolfsburg…Joselu joins Deportivo…Berahino deal (£20m) falls through…Bruno Martins-Indi and Wilfried Bony sign-up on loan. Bringing in Bony a "no brainier", says Hughes, "let's just enjoy him")

14/08/2016
Trouserdog@TrouserdogSCFC

Goodbye Wilson. You were half decent at left back for a few months in 2011 and kept Tom Hanks company on that island

---

16/08/2016
Will@IamWillSCFC

The fact that Phillip Wollscheid hasn't got a chant to the tune of Mr Brightside saddens me….

16/08/2016
Espleypotter@Marcespley

What a kick in the teeth if Joe Hart signs for Stoke and becomes number 2 at club and country

---

19/08/2016
Will@IamWillSCFC

If Hughes is being truthful and we have no specific transfer targets at this point in the window, we want fucking.

19/08/2016
Dave@davematthews79

Can Stoke sign the GBR hockey keeper Maddie Hinch on loan to cover for Butland? What a keeper! Miles better than Haugaard! #teamGB

20/08/2016
Dorset potter@cain_rosscain

Dear Sparky please say that sitting by the phone waiting for Tony to ring was not your only plan to get a striker 😨

25/08/2016
HAIRY POTTER@cosnakickbo

@wildog87 I turn my back for one second you've signed for Bournemouth, Scored a Goal and started Smiling 🍜🍺👍

27/08/2016
Dorset potter@cain_rosscain

Dear M H You do know that defenders and strikers won't come knocking on your door .Youve actually got to go and find them before Wed 😨😨

27/08/2016
DUCK MAGAZINE@DUCKmagstoke

The manager has more than enough in the bank not to be getting some of the stick he has in last 7 days. But we need to buy, that's for sure

27/08/2016
David Cowlishaw@davidcowlishaw

I seriously worry that our local media never ask anything of importance to Hughes.

28/08/2016
HAIRY POTTER@cosnakickbo

The Social Media Natives are Getting Restless 😂😂😂 We However 😄😄😄 :-) #stokecity

28/08/2016
Espleypotter@Marcespley

The scenes when WBA finally release Berahino on deadline day and he fails his medical at Stoke

30/08/2016
Will@IamWillSCFC

Has the bloke doing the updates on the @stokecity Twitter feed fallen asleep or has absolutely nowt happened for 10 minutes?

30/08/2016
Rob Doolan@ChiefDelilah

Easily the worst thing about being a Stoke fan on deadline day is all the pizza jokes. Get some new material lads.

30/08/2016
Will@IamWillSCFC

The state of this transfer window! You spend 10 years getting promotion, becoming a top half PL club and fucking ruin it over one Summer!

31/08/2016
Martin Smith@SolarSmudge

Me on transfer deadline day, praying that Stoke sign someone! #scfc #TransferDeadline #brickingit

31/08/2016
Will@IamWillSCFC

It's time to find out if the pizza boys have played an absolute blinder or if they've been completely reckless #DeadlineDay

31/08/2016
Rob Doolan@ChiefDelilah

Delighted with Bony. Hope we're lining up late moves for Drut, Berk & The Thing Upstairs #dontyouopenthattrapdoor

31/08/2016
Will@IamWillSCFC

Woke up feeling completely hopeless about our club. A few hours later I'm bouncing, dreaming about the next one in #DeadlineDay

31/08/2016
David Lee@stoke_city_pub

Stoke City sign the blacklisted Hollywood starlet Lee Grant on loan till January...oh, hang on, that's not right... #scfc

31/08/2016
Dave@davematthews79

Not too arsed about Wolly going. Occasionally good but questionable temperament and turned like the Titanic. Good luck to the guy though.

31/08/2016
Dave@davematthews79

Pleased with our deals, can't wait to see Bony up front. Then again, I remember thinking how amazing Dave Kitson would be, so what do I know

31/08/2016
Espleypotter@Marcespley

Note the media team don't sign players, Mark Hughes does not sign players. Scholes signs the players

31/08/2016
Will@IamWillSCFC

And the other bonus of signing Wilfried Bony that no is talking about, is that he comes with his own ready made song #winwin

31/08/2016
Espleypotter@Marcespley

Stoke signing Bony has no reflection on us signing Saido. We are still after Berahino

31/08/2016
Dorset potter@cain_rosscain

If we end up with Bony and leave Baggies stuck with Berahino I will s-t myself laughing 😅😅😅😅

31/08/2016
Martin Smith@SolarSmudge

Wilfreid Bony... We happy? Yeah, we happy! #SCFC #transferdeadline

02/09/2016
Will@IamWillSCFC

This Butland injury is an absolute disaster. Can we just get to 40 points please and try again next season?

03/09/2016
Trouserdog@TrouserdogSCFC

I'm lost without football on Saturday afternoons. Laughing at Vale getting dicked in the rain doesn't count.

08/09/2016
Will@IamWillSCFC

The enigma that is Shaqiri. Can play 3 games in a week for his country yet strains every known muscle lacing his boots in Stoke-on-Trent

20/09/2016
David Lee@stoke_city_pub

Mark Bowen defiant about Marc Wilson's tweet criticising Stoke's defensive training. "He's entitled to his opinion."

10/09/2016
Will@IamWillSCFC

Any idea what name Martins Indi wears on his shirt? Little un wants "the man with the funny eyes" on his new away shirt

10/09/2016   **Stoke City (0) 0 Spurs (1) 4**

(Oh dear. Stoke lose to Spurs by 4 goals...again...and again! Sparky gets sent to the stands (for tip-toeing inches out of his technical area), then struggles to get a phone signal up there - much like everyone else. Arnie's early goal is disallowed, then it just goes downhill from there...again. Spurs fans merrily sing ""It's happening again...!"" New first-starts Wilfried Bony and Bruno Martins Indi must be wondering what they've signed up for!)

Premier League position: 20th

Order on MotD: 4th out of 8

10/09/2016
Will@IamWillSCFC

Quietly optimistic about today's game #GoOnStoke

10/09/2016
DUCK MAGAZINE@DUCKmagstoke

Spurs not sold out? Must be saving money for new elastic-bottomed maroon skinny jeans.

10/09/2016
David Cowlishaw@davidcowlishaw

In the same way Wollscheid was rounded on for not being Huth, Imbula is being rounded on for not being N'Zonzi.

10/09/2016
Danny Bowers@dannybowers10

Ref books arnie for a dive, alli & son dive, no yellow. @fa You're very consistent at being awful every week.

10/09/2016
David Lee@stoke_city_pub

Commentator: "Hope Mark Hughes gets a good phone signal. This place not renowned for good mobile signal!"

10/09/2016
David Cowlishaw@davidcowlishaw

Mark Hughes is basing his tactics on the episode of The Simpsons where Homer becomes a boxer and keeps getting punched in the face.

10/09/2016
Rob Doolan@ChiefDelilah

Can't help but feel that Hughes has got himself into a mess with the Imbula/Allen situation.

10/09/2016
Espleypotter@Marcespley

Pieters has to be dropped now, simple as

10/09/2016
David Lee@stoke_city_pub

There can be NO excuses about injuries. We are just still poor from last season.

10/09/2016
Will@IamWillSCFC

Bojan is our star man. The team should be built around him. And Bardsley has been our best defender. Having them on the bench was criminal

10/09/2016
David Cowlishaw@davidcowlishaw

Imbula is actually having a decent game. Not that that will matter to some.

10/09/2016
DUCK MAGAZINE@DUCKmagstoke

Fair play to the lads, they eventually managed to make the ref look like he had a decent game. Some doing.

10/09/2016
David Cowlishaw@davidcowlishaw

The lengths we'll go to in order to shoehorn our worst player.

10/09/2016
The Oatcake Fanzine@oatcakescfc

A very worrying performance. Spurs are a good team, but we shouldn't be rolled over that easily on our own ground. We're creating nothing.

10/09/2016
David Lee@stoke_city_pub

You could bet your house on where Pulis' WBA would be (13th). But Mark Hughes' QPR look in trouble (20th). Er, I mean Stoke. #blip

10/09/2016
HAIRY POTTER@cosnakickbo

To Me You Shouldn't be Talkingabout a Referee but it's Every Match #SparkysinTheStand

10/09/2016
David Cowlishaw@davidcowlishaw

Fuck supporting Spurs, Man City, Man U, Chelsea, Arsenal etc. Your team losing 4-0 at home makes you a better person. It just does.

10/09/2016
DUCK MAGAZINE@DUCKmagstoke

26 conceded in last 10 league games? That right? Wow. I mean, WOW!

10/09/2016
BadManners@BringontheHippo

I can handle losing. It's the amount conceded and lack of chances created I have an issue with. Just don't understand our plan.

10/09/2016
David Cowlishaw@davidcowlishaw

Who should replace Hughes then?

11/09/2016
Dorset potter@cain_rosscain

Spurs beat us 4-0 last season well done thats down to your skill .This season is down to us learning sod all from last season 😢 😢 😢

12/09/2016
Rob Doolan@ChiefDelilah

I've seen a number of suggestions that Hughes has 'taken us backwards' from where we were. Reminder that this is a load of cock.

13/09/2016
Dorset potter@cain_rosscain

Why is' Homes Under the Hammer 'always in stoke . What are they trying to say 😐

14/09/2016
Rob Doolan@ChiefDelilah

In light of Phil Jones' injury and Berahino's sluggishness, you wonder if we might have got incredibly lucky this transfer window.

14/09/2016
Will@IamWillSCFC

Happy Clappers as Stoke sit bottom of the league, no clean sheet in 21 league games, and creating absolutely nowt

16/09/2016
David Lee@stoke_city_pub

Very impressed with Mark Hughes at today's #scfc press conference.
Handled himself with dignity, whilst serving an ace past the FA.

16/09/2016
Terry Conroy@TerryConroy

After our victory at Palace on Sunday,life will be a lot rosier.!!

18/09/2016   Crystal Palace (2) 4 Stoke City (0) 1

(Stoke's worst start to a season just gets worse. The first 12 minutes are appalling, with Stoke going 0-2 down, and then it just goes downhill… well, you get the idea of that. Arnie scores in time-added, and not only that it's from open-play! But the knives are out.)

Premier League position: 20th

Order on MotD: 2nd out of 4

17/09/2016
David Lee@stoke_city_pub

Stoke City have lost 5 out of the last 6 games against Crystal Palace, with the 6th game a draw. But Sparky won there with ManCity…

18/09/2016
David Cowlishaw@davidcowlishaw

BOJAN STARTS *Cheers erupt* SO DOES WALTERS *boos* WE'RE 4-2-3-1 *cheers* IMBULA DROPPED *boos* PIETERS DROPPED *cheers* BMI AT LB *boos*

18/09/2016
Rob Doolan@ChiefDelilah

Stoke XI looks like a step forward, for the most part.

18/09/2016
Trouserdog@TrouserdogSCFC

If I openly slag off the selection of Walters on here, that guarantees he'll play a blinder, right? FFS Hughes, Walters is wank. #GooarnJon

---

18/09/2016
Rob Doolan@ChiefDelilah

Who's booing Imbula being dropped? Mrs Imbula?

18/09/2016
Trouserdog@TrouserdogSCFC

Pieters finally being dropped warrants the champagne coming out of the booze cupboard. I've been searching for a reason for ages...

18/09/2016
DUCK MAGAZINE@DUCKmagstoke

I've always thought we do anger far better than love, at Stoke Whilst noone's happy, & quite right too, I for one can not wait for Saturday

18/09/2016
Rob Doolan@ChiefDelilah

2-0 down and yet Bony couldn't be more isolated if he was marooned on a desert island with only a volleyball for company.

18/09/2016
Danny Bowers@dannybowers10

Unnatural left back, Walters on the wing again, getting far too regular this is.

18/09/2016
Rob Doolan@ChiefDelilah

Maybe we could do some defensive training the players DO know they're doing Sparky?

18/09/2016
Dorset potter@cain_rosscain

don't think we were that bad under pulis, really worried about us now, this wants to be some half time talk

18/09/2016
Rob Doolan@ChiefDelilah

Jon Walters' fabled defensive qualities coming up trumps again...

18/09/2016
Danny Bowers@dannybowers10

Two set pieces, two goals. All that talk and shown nothing on the pitch again.

18/09/2016
Trouserdog@TrouserdogSCFC

How the fuck are Spurs not 5 up?

18/09/2016
The Oatcake Fanzine@oatcakescfc

Even by our wretched standards at Selhurst Park that was pitiful. A completely unacceptable performance. We are a mess. #SCFC

18/09/2016
Trouserdog@TrouserdogSCFC

@mspinks10 Wouldn't win you favour with the club, but just writing 'useless, disorganised wankers' 1000 times would capture that performance

18/09/2016
Dorset potter@cain_rosscain

We are now the premiere league laughing stock' how long till we play Stoke' it really is all over Sparky sorry 😕

18/09/2016
DUCK MAGAZINE@DUCKmagstoke

Players should be getting their share too. It's not just the manager here. That team is easily good enough with anyone managing it.

18/09/2016
Neil Finney@NeilFinney

Team lacked direction and identity today. Serious stuff. Its not player combinations. Deeper than that. #scfc

18/09/2016
Will@IamWillSCFC

In the last 2 games we've conceded 8 goals. In the same time, Phil "the weak link" Wollscheid has kept 2 clean sheets with Wolfsburg 👍

18/09/2016
Espleypotter@Marcespley

We can kind of except conceding 4 against ManCity and Spurs, but Palace!!! We need to start well and we are not doing, we cannot chase

18/09/2016
Will@IamWillSCFC

I've said it once, I'll say it again! Thank fuck we got rid of Wollscheid....

18/09/2016
DUCK MAGAZINE@DUCKmagstoke

I'm not one for refunding away fans.....but those who went Palace on a Sunday for this???

18/09/2016
Will@IamWillSCFC

Alright Pete, you know that £25 million you put aside for Berahino? Use it now to get a manager in who knows what he's doing please

18/09/2016
David Cowlishaw@davidcowlishaw

I'd honestly rather we went down than Pulis came back

18/09/2016
Espleypotter@Marcespley

I cannot see us winning a game again under Hughes. We just cannot defend

18/09/2016
DUCK MAGAZINE@DUCKmagstoke

Undercooked preseason? Fitness levels? Slowest team in the league? Overanalysing or valid thoughts?

18/09/2016
Clive Bickley@Bickers1952

Since Feb 21 games W5 D4 L12 F20 A47 19 from 63 points! 3 times on trot lost 3-0 6x 4 goal defeats. Is this not relegation form?

18/09/2016
Dorset potter@cain_rosscain

We are now at a point where a win won't get us out of the relegation places

19/09/2016
Trouserdog@TrouserdogSCFC

I think Radio Stoke should do an interview with Denise, where all she does is scream "Aaaaaaxxxeeee" like some sort of crazed banshee

19/09/2016
Will@IamWillSCFC

Hughes should walk today. The vitriol on Saturday when West Brom dick us will be like nothing he's ever witnessed

19/09/2016
Trouserdog@TrouserdogSCFC

Coates sounded crankier than my Mrs when it's time of the month...I reckon he's stroking the axe now to calm down.

20/09/2016
HAIRY POTTER@cosnakickbo

"The goal never moves so it's all about hitting the target" Message MH We Need Find It !!! TP's on his Way #Saturday Listen & Learn 🥣🏺👍

21/09/2016   Stoke City (1) 1 Hull City (1) 2

(More like it for Stoke...but their first-team still lose easily at home to a seriously-understrength Hull. Arnie hits a cracker to make it 1-0, Hull equalise on half-time, and win it in the 91st minute. First starts for brilliant Ramadan Sobhi and credible goalie Lee Grant are overshadowed by the fact that Stoke, well, just aren't any good.)

21/09/2016
HAIRY POTTER@cosnakickbo

There's a Joke going around "What Time is It ? " "4 past Stoke" 😂😂😂
Time to put that one to Bed !!!

21/09/2016
Martin Smith@SolarSmudge

We should be Three up and, of bloody course, they score with their first shot at goal right on half-time. Typical Stoke. #scfc #eplcup

---

21/09/2016
Trouserdog@TrouserdogSCFC

Freak result that. Dominated from start to finish yet somehow lost. Think Sparky must have run over a black cat and broke all his mirrors.

21/09/2016
The Oatcake Fanzine@oatcakescfc

Those who were dishing out the abuse to Ryan in the DPD Stand tonight should do us all a favour a go and play on the M6 on Saturday.

21/09/2016
Dave@davematthews79

That game seemed so difficult to lose but somehow we managed it! Classic Stoke 😡

21/09/2016
The Oatcake Fanzine@oatcakescfc

Another depressing #SCFC experience. We're a walking, talking hard luck story at the moment. Struggling to see what we're trying to do.

21/09/2016
Danny Bowers@dannybowers10

Much better performance today and a lot more positives, Sobhi has to start vs West Brom.

21/09/2016
Espleypotter@Marcespley

All I can say is if Walters plays ahead of Sobhi then someone needs shooting. Sobhi was quality tonight, pity our finishing wasn't

22/09/2016
David Cowlishaw@davidcowlishaw

Never been more convinced that we'll beat West Brom. The melts.

23/09/2016
Neil Finney@NeilFinney

I bet the Sentinel has some good Stoke City news stories but I really can't be bothered fending off all the adverts.

24/09/2016   **Stoke City (0) 1 WBA (0) 1**

(Strangely, this is the turning point. Pulis was never going to lose this one; he's beaten Stoke every time since he left, so a draw is a major breakthrough! Joe Allen scores on 73, but it's typical heartbreak as Rondon heads home Albion's equaliser from an unnecessary corner in injury time.)

Premier League position: 19th

Order on MotD: 8th out of 8

24/09/2016
BadManners@BringontheHippo

a clean sheet would make my weekend. 1-0 stoke

24/09/2016
The Oatcake Fanzine@oatcakescfc

Pulis: "They have an array of talent that we haven't got". Have a day off Tony, you've spent as much as Hughes in your time as WBA manager.

24/09/2016
Will@IamWillSCFC

So was today a 'must win' or a 'must have more possession whilst creating very little'?

24/09/2016
Neil Finney@NeilFinney

more disappointment today but looked better. Remaining positive..

24/09/2016
Will@IamWillSCFC

Not as convinced as others by today's performance. We still created next to nothing and paid the price with more comedy defending

24/09/2016
David Lee@stoke_city_pub

Tony Pulis & Mark Hughes shake hands as only they know how. #scfc #wba #freemasons #Celts #peoplewhodontlikeeachothermuch

24/09/2016
Danny Bowers@dannybowers10

Sobhi completely out the squad?! Is that what you deserve after a motm performance?

24/09/2016
DUCK MAGAZINE@DUCKmagstoke

Major concern for me from today's game was Coldplay blaring out when the lads ran out second half.

24/09/2016
David Cowlishaw@davidcowlishaw

Hughes out. 100%.

24/09/2016
Martin Smith@SolarSmudge

On a positive note, that performance from Joe Allen was immense. Easily the best player on the pitch! Just superb. #SCFC #joeallen

25/09/2016
Trouserdog@TrouserdogSCFC

I thought we were loose at the back; West Ham are doubly incontinent.

25/09/2016
Neil Finney@NeilFinney

Hughes must remain in charge. Far to early for change. Some big, winnable home games coming up.

02/10/2016   Manchester United (0) 1 Stoke City (0) 1

(Finally, Stoke get a result at Old Trafford for the first time in 36 years... well, it might as well be a 100 years. Martial looks like he's won it for United, before Joe Allen pokes home the equaliser in the 82nd to take Stoke off the bottom of the League. Mourinho is not amused. Well, he never is.)

Premier League position: 19th

Order on MotD: 2nd out of 4

30/09/2016
David Lee@stoke_city_pub

A sneezing, unshaven Mark Hughes hopes he's out of the woods with injuries now Shaq & GlenJ are back. #scfc #pressConference

---

02/10/2016
David Cowlishaw@davidcowlishaw

Why the hell did Liverpool sell Joe Allen? The man is incredible.

02/10/2016
Rob Doolan@ChiefDelilah

Crystal Palace were two up by this point. #progress

02/10/2016
David Cowlishaw@davidcowlishaw

Incredible that Ibrahimovic can't convert a chance Kyle Lightbourne would have tucked away.

02/10/2016
Rob Doolan@ChiefDelilah

A lot of the heart and fight that's been absent to this point shown by Stoke, even if we're a shade fortunate to have made it to half time.

02/10/2016
HAIRY POTTER@cosnakickbo

Chicken Oriental The Mental just Finished at HP's Give Me Hope Joe Allen Hope Joe Allen I'm City Til My Dying Day ⛲⛲⛲

02/10/2016
DUCK MAGAZINE@DUCKmagstoke

Big fan of being in love with Joe Allen, me. Big fan.

02/10/2016
David Cowlishaw@davidcowlishaw

Zlatan shut down by Shawcross. Joe Allen fucking everywhere. Lee Grant an adonis. I LOVE YOU STOKE.

02/10/2016
Rob Doolan@ChiefDelilah

Lee Grant, be my wife.

02/10/2016
HAIRY POTTER@cosnakickbo

YOU BEAUTIES MOM Lee Grant GOALSCORER Joe Allen #MUNSTK

02/10/2016
Martin Smith@SolarSmudge

Joe Allen... £15m Paul Pogba... £89m We live in strange times! #mufcvsscfc #pogba #JoeAllen #stokecity

02/10/2016
David Cowlishaw@davidcowlishaw

Good, gutsy performance. Bony not working like Diouf does. Arnie utter class. Grant is Gordon Banks reincarnate.

02/10/2016
Neil Finney@NeilFinney

Did that Herrera tackle deserve a red card? Not so sure as the ref could clearly see his red Utd shirt. #playonlads

02/10/2016
HAIRY POTTER@cosnakickbo

DEFFO RED CARD "He Plays for Stoke You Send Him Off"

02/10/2016
HAIRY POTTER@cosnakickbo

SEEING RED Herrera Studs Allen Just a Yellow

02/10/2016
David Cowlishaw@davidcowlishaw

Could have brought Sobhi and Bojan on. No? Oh fine, these barely Championship quality cloggers will suffice.

02/10/2016
David Cowlishaw@davidcowlishaw

BT commentator in banter mode: "Why have Stoke dressed up like Man City lol" It's our away kit you prick.

02/10/2016
Trouserdog@TrouserdogSCFC

Can't believe how Imbula's gone from looking like a mini-Yaya Toure to being behind Charlie Adam in the pecking order. £18m down the bog.

02/10/2016
Rob Doolan@ChiefDelilah

His subs almost seem like performance art now. Like Les Dawson playing the piano deliberately badly.

02/10/2016
HAIRY POTTER@cosnakickbo

Screams of Give it ARNIE From Dot age 84 down the Road

02/10/2016
The Oatcake Fanzine@oatcakescfc

Brilliant result for Stoke. Certainly rode our luck, but a great show of character. Grant was absolutely outstanding and Allen again superb.

02/10/2016
Chris Ault@Chrisa020985

First time I've smiled all season! Mourinho had the look of someone who had just caught his wife in bed with John Terry.

02/10/2016
Danny Bowers@dannybowers10

What a performance from Stoke today, every player fought for the team.

02/10/2016
Clive Bickley@Bickers1952

Super result but when are officials going to play on a level playing field with us. Why were Herrera and Pogba not sent off?

03/10/2016
Will@IamWillSCFC

Every dickhead and his dog spewing bile about Glen Johnson's re-call by England. But not one suggestion of who else it should have been

08/10/2016
Chris Ault@Chrisa020985

How the hell does @Charlie26Adam not get picked for Scotland? #disgrace

08/10/2016
Trouserdog@TrouserdogSCFC

FIFA 17 is going on ebay. I've gone from being decent at 16 to the gaming equivalent of Keith Scott. Getting dicked every game. :-(

12/10/2016
Clive Bickley@Bickers1952

When is someone up there going to smile on us and put an end to this ridiculous catalogue of injuries. #frustratingnothalf

14/10/2016
Will@IamWillSCFC

The first year in my adult life that I've got Christmas Day and Boxing Day off work and them tossers @SkySports move the match #clueless

15/10/2016   Stoke City (2) 2 Sunderland (0) 0

(""Two first half goals for Stoke"" is a phrase that hasn't been heard for a long time at Stoke, but Joe Allen obliges with a brace in this must-win-October-bottom-of-the-league-clash. The question is, if David Moyes can't win here, where can he win?? Bless.)

Premier League position: 18th

Order on MotD: 6th out of 7

14/10/2016
David Cowlishaw@davidcowlishaw

We need to win tomorrow. Glad I'm not going, I can't cope.

15/10/2016
Trouserdog@TrouserdogSCFC

Oi! Stoke! No fucking about today- 3 points urgently needed. Sunderland are shite so no excuses.

15/10/2016
Rob Doolan@ChiefDelilah

Reassuring to know that in these troubled times for the clowning industry, Martin Atkinson keeps on keeping on.

15/10/2016
Rob Doolan@ChiefDelilah

The Sunderland bench, brought to you by the earth year 2009.

15/10/2016
Will@IamWillSCFC

How poor were Sunderland? One tactic of twatting the ball up to a 4ft Defoe and that was it. Dreadful team, dreadful tactics #goingdown

---

15/10/2016
Rob Doolan@ChiefDelilah

Ok, 10 minutes. Just got to not do anything stupid. I'm looking at you Erik/Geoff/Charlie…

15/10/2016
Espleypotter@Marcespley

Martins Indi looks solid and beginning to get an understanding with Shawcross. Glad we have an option to sign already sorted

15/10/2016
Rob Doolan@ChiefDelilah

It wouldn't be a match day without at least one screaming mental substitution.

15/10/2016
Trouserdog@TrouserdogSCFC

I'm developing feelings for Joe Allen. Feelings that I've never had before for another man (apart from Ricardo Fuller, Hoekstra and Steino)

15/10/2016
DUCK MAGAZINE@DUCKmagstoke

…and on the seventh day, Joe Allen created God

15/10/2016
Will@IamWillSCFC

Just to put things into perspective. Joe Allen's goals have earned us 5 of our 6 points so far this season, that's 83.3% #noallenoparty

15/10/2016
Rob Doolan@ChiefDelilah

Enjoying Sunderland's away kit

15/10/2016
David Lee@stoke_city_pub

Great! Disciplined! Thankfully we weren't playing anybody good…

15/10/2016
DUCK MAGAZINE@DUCKmagstoke

Joe Allen doesn't walk on water, he just allows it to flow under his feet

15/10/2016
Will@IamWillSCFC

Lee Grant, didn't have much to do, but it's amazing how well a defence play when they have faith in the man behind them #signhimup

15/10/2016
Dorset potter@cain_rosscain

Anyone explain what Sunderland thought they would get from high long balls into the box Defoe 5ft Shawcross 6ft plus ??? W T F

15/10/2016
Will@IamWillSCFC

if Diouf had linked up with players and won everything like Bony did, he wouldn't be on the bench

15/10/2016
DUCK MAGAZINE@DUCKmagstoke

Yes, Allen was brilliant again, but Geoff Cameron was my MOTM. Immense from first whistle

15/10/2016
DUCK MAGAZINE@DUCKmagstoke

Fair play to Sunderland team….last 3 years they've all been out after the game signing stuff for kids. Sounds nowt, but means a lot.

15/10/2016
Will@IamWillSCFC

I've been hard on him this season, but Ryan was back to his old self today. Strong, vocal, decisive, much better from our captain

15/10/2016
DUCK MAGAZINE@DUCKmagstoke

Almost 20 years on, traffic after a game still a nightmare

15/10/2016
Espleypotter@Marcespley

Second to last on MOTD, we are improving

16/10/2016
Terry Conroy@TerryConroy

At long last,3 points.Lots of good performances,Allen,as usual,outstanding.I thought Bony's hold up play terrific,first goal so close now

22/10/2016   Hull City (0) 0 Stoke City (1) 2

(Another two goals, these ones by Shaqiri! But like Sunderland, this is a very poor side, even poorer than Stoke and Sunderland! Interestingly, this full-strength Hull side at home isn't as good as the part-timers who beat Stoke away a couple of weeks ago...)

Premier League position: 16th

Order on MotD: 4th out of 8

22/10/2016
DUCK MAGAZINE@DUCKmagstoke

Mike Phelan, looking like the third, more poorly dressed Chuckle Brother

---

22/10/2016
Espleypotter@Marcespley

Great from Shawcross for Stoke's second. Moves wall and ducks to allow Shaq's free kick to pass through wall

---

22/10/2016
David Cowlishaw@davidcowlishaw

Me and football are mates again. Only took a couple of Shaq pingers to do it.

22/10/2016
The Oatcake Fanzine@oatcakescfc

A special mention to the loony tune Hull fan who rang in to @RadioHumberside to proclaim Stoke as the worst Premier League team he'd seen. 😂

22/10/2016
Espleypotter@Marcespley

I see the ref made up for his mistake in the game of not booking a Stoke player. 3 booked in the tunnel

22/10/2016
The Oatcake Fanzine@oatcakescfc

As comfortable an away day we've had since promotion. Stoke in control comfortably and worthy of a much better victory. #SCFC

22/10/2016
Chris Ault@Chrisa020985

That's more like it @stokecity onwards and upwards

22/10/2016
Espleypotter@Marcespley

You wait for months for a clean sheet, then 2 come along after each other

22/10/2016
HAIRY POTTER@cosnakickbo

I BELIEVE in @wilfriedbony #GoWilf GOALS GOALS GOALS #TodaysTheDay 🍀🍀🍀🍀

22/10/2016
DUCK MAGAZINE@DUCKmagstoke

Who put Rooney on the kitchen floor, Super Philip Bardsley

22/10/2016
Neil Finney@NeilFinney

We know Bony will get his goal soon probably against Swansea and Swansea know it too #scfc

23/10/2016
Terry Conroy@TerryConroy

it could have been 6, with Arnies & Bonys chances.!

23/10/2016
David Cowlishaw@davidcowlishaw

Man City in 'crisis' and still top of the league. They're winning this title comfortably.

23/10/2016
Terry Conroy@TerryConroy

Shaq on fire yesterday,fire brigade not need,only our pocket dynamo showing his exceptional skills to destroy Hull,great to watch

25/10/2016
Trouserdog@TrouserdogSCFC

Me and FIFA 17 are spending some time apart. We need our own space.

28/10/2016
David Lee@stoke_city_pub

Mark Hughes' record as a manager vs Swansea: 3 wins, 3 draws, 2 lost. Home record: 2W, 2D, 1L. (The latter a 0-5 loss at QPR). #scfc

30/10/2016
The Oatcake Fanzine@oatcakescfc

Look out for our new series in tomorrow night's Oatcake... "Norman Smurthwaite's Tweets of the Week"... this one could run and run!

31/10/2016   Stoke City (1) 3 Swansea City (1) 1

(THREE goals! For Stoke! In front of the Sky cameras! Another poor side is seen off by Stoke, as Stoke go from strength to strength. Ex-Swans Joe Allen and Bony tear Swansea apart. However, poor Wilfried, finally on the score sheet, never scores for Stoke again.)

Premier League position: 12th

Order on MotD: (N/A)

31/10/2016
HAIRY POTTER@cosnakickbo

Darkness Falls Across the Land, The Kick Off Hours Close at Hand #ScaryPotter #STKSWA #MNF #halloween 🎃🎃🎃

31/10/2016
Will@IamWillSCFC

I for one don't mind the line up. Unsettling a winning team would be mental. Cameron is injured, so Adam is the easiest replacement

---

31/10/2016
David Cowlishaw@davidcowlishaw

Been a while since I've been the Bet365. Come on you useless tossers, score more goals than the other team.

31/10/2016
David Lee@stoke_city_pub

Loving watching new boys Bony, Allen, Ramadan, Grant & Martins-Indi. Plus Arnie & Charlie. Great #scfc team. #STOSWA

31/10/2016
David Cowlishaw@davidcowlishaw

A slapstick first half followed by a professional second half. Allen great, Sobhi great, Pieters...jesus christ.

31/10/2016
David Cowlishaw@davidcowlishaw

Charlie Adam, the immobile ball dispenser. Great feet, shame he can't run on them.

31/10/2016
The Oatcake Fanzine@oatcakescfc

Excellent from Stoke, 5 or 6 goals would've done that performance justice. Livid about Arnie's card. A shameful decision from Oliver. #SCFC

31/10/2016
Will@IamWillSCFC

The beautiful thing might be that the support shown to Wilf through his dry spell is what makes a 20 goals a season striker sign for us

31/10/2016
Espleypotter@Marcespley

We are missing Cameron

31/10/2016
David Cowlishaw@davidcowlishaw

You know, people were perfectly within their rights to call for Hughes to go after Palace.

01/11/2016
DUCK MAGAZINE@DUCKmagstoke

Honestly thought Charlie Adam must have packed in international football. How can he not walk into their team, never mind squad?

05/11/2016   West Ham United (0) 1 Stoke City (0) 1

(Stoke now proving hard to beat, Whelan's own goal is put right by a Bardsley-Walters move that is finished off by sub Bojan. Sparky's Stoke is fast becoming a right bogey side for The Hammers, unbeaten in 7.)

Premier League position: 12th

Order on MotD: 5th out of 5

02/11/2016
David Lee@stoke_city_pub

Mark Hughes' record at West Ham is not great: only one win in 9 games. However, he's unbeaten in his last 4 games there. #scfc

---

05/11/2016
Will@IamWillSCFC

For the second week running, all this outrage about Bojan not playing. Where exactly should he be playing?! On the wing?!

06/11/2016
Dave@davematthews79

Dunno whether to laugh at the Hammers fans misfortune or feel sorry for them

---

05/11/2016
DUCK MAGAZINE@DUCKmagstoke

We're closer to Euston than we are to Erik Pieters

05/11/2016
David Cowlishaw@davidcowlishaw

I love Bojan.

05/11/2016
Will@IamWillSCFC

This has been an awful spectacle so far. #lastonMotD

05/11/2016
DUCK MAGAZINE@DUCKmagstoke

West Ham shot ends up in long jump pit

05/11/2016
DUCK MAGAZINE@DUCKmagstoke

"We like your trampolines"

05/11/2016
Will@IamWillSCFC

I'll put this out there. When Jack is fit, he's not guaranteed to start. The shirt is Lee Grant's to lose. Top save from him again today

05/11/2016
Trouserdog@TrouserdogSCFC

Going to celebrate today's point with a vindaloo. To be honest that's also how I would have celebrated a win, or taken solace in defeat.

05/11/2016
Will@IamWillSCFC

"All the danger for Stoke has come down the right hand side through Jon Walters" but still Stoke Twitter knows best 😂

05/11/2016
Rob Doolan@ChiefDelilah

Can't be long before Mike Dean's playing Frank N'Furter on the West End.

05/11/2016
The Oatcake Fanzine@oatcakescfc

Deserved point for The Potters. Sparky has a real headache now with so many players in form. Really impressed with Ramadan. #SCFC

17/11/2016
Will@IamWillSCFC

Joe Allen's hair on Fifa is nothing short of a disgrace

17/11/2016
Will@IamWillSCFC

Do @EA genuinely believe that Glenn Whelan looks like that freak that they keep wheeling out as him every year on Fifa?

18/11/2016
David Lee@stoke_city_pub

Despite me reiterating fans' loathing for international breaks, Mark Hughes declines my offer to lead movement against them! #pressconference

19/11/2016 Stoke City (0) 0 Bournemouth (1) 1

(A litmus-test game for Stoke against a side they did the double over the previous season. There are just too many well-organised mid-table sides and ""Boscombe"" are but one. A goal from a free header when surrounded by 11 Stoke players speaks volumes, but then Bojan blazing a penalty off towards the Michelin factory mutters away several more!)

Premier League position: 13th

Order on MotD: 7th out of 8

19/11/2016
David Cowlishaw@davidcowlishaw

Bojan missing a penalty is worse than Trump, Brexit and Harambe.

19/11/2016
Dorset potter@cain_rosscain

Guys I'd like to point out I live and work amongst Bournemouth fans don't make me go to work Mon on the loosing side

---

19/11/2016
Espleypotter@Marcespley

Bournemouth players spent more time rolling around than the ball did. Shocking display

---

19/11/2016
Will@IamWillSCFC

wouldn't have scored if we were still playing now. Bournemouth biggest bunch of shithouses to come down Stoke since WBA last year

---

19/11/2016
David Lee@stoke_city_pub

How is the Bournemouth goalkeeper allowed to play in the same colors as the referees?! #wtf

19/11/2016
Danny Bowers@dannybowers10

Why Sobhi has been dropped for this drivel is beyond me. Allen, Adam & bojan are not working.

19/11/2016
David Cowlishaw@davidcowlishaw

Bournemouth were a set of pricks, ref was shite and we were insipid. Bloody love football, me.

19/11/2016
David Lee@stoke_city_pub

It was like a League 1 side vs a Championship side.

19/11/2016
David Cowlishaw@davidcowlishaw

Nobody had a good game, but in my Room 101 is a 90minute player cam of Charlie Adam today. Utter shite.

19/11/2016
Neil Finney@NeilFinney

Ref at Stoke was dreadful from start to finish. Got just about everything wrong. Including the Bournemouth pen not given. Awful stuff.

19/11/2016
David Lee@stoke_city_pub

We just have to accept that the flair players are NOTHING without the likes of Whelan & Cameron. It was like watching ME play football! Ugh!

19/11/2016

David Cowlishaw@davidcowlishaw

Our midfield is being walked through. Nobody playing above 6/10 at the moment.

19/11/2016

DUCK MAGAZINE@DUCKmagstoke

Most worrying thing today is how knackered we've looked. Leggy from first minute

19/11/2016

The Oatcake Fanzine@oatcakescfc

These people having a go at Rooney need to wind their necks in. Have you ever played with a hangover?

19/11/2016

Neil Finney@NeilFinney

I thought nil nils were usually last on #motd #boredraw #sotliv

19/11/2016

Espleypotter@Marcespley

Despite Imbula not been able to tackle, he should of played over Adam, as today showed Adam cannot do anything never mind tackle

19/11/2016

Terry Conroy@TerryConroy

Even though we missed a pen and Shakiri chance,they were far better than us.Pace and movement in abundance

20/11/2016

Espleypotter@Marcespley

Bournemouth played well first half, hard press and created space well when on the ball.Hate to say it Wilshere ran the midfield

27/11/2016   Watford (0) 0 Stoke City (1) 1

(Hard to say who was more surprised by Stoke coming fast out of the blocks at Watford: Stoke fans? Sparky? Or shell-shocked Watford players? Charlie Adam causes mayhem in the box causing goalie Gomez to concede an own goal. All this shock and mayhem is capped by Imbula returning and having a decent game!)

Premier League position: 11th

Order on MotD: 4th out of 4

27/11/2016
David Cowlishaw@davidcowlishaw

Back 3? Really?

27/11/2016
Dorset potter@cain_rosscain

I know there are some forced changes but also some tinkering this better bloody work 😐

27/11/2016
HAIRY POTTER@cosnakickbo

Watford Sing 1-0 to The Referee but it's STOKE GET IN !!!

27/11/2016
Rob Doolan@ChiefDelilah

Don't quite understand our reticence to making subs, but that is a great win without the captain or our entire first choice midfield.

27/11/2016
The Oatcake Fanzine@oatcakescfc

Our best performance of the season from the most cobbled together team! Great response to AFCB defeat, shows we have good strength in depth.

27/11/2016
Will@IamWillSCFC

Bizarre line up, brilliant performance. Well done Mark Hughes! Superb Stoke!

27/11/2016
DUCK MAGAZINE@DUCKmagstoke

Hughes got it absolutely spot on today.

27/11/2016
Espleypotter@Marcespley

.@MameDiouf99 attempted and won 5 tackles v Watford. 3 more than any other Stoke player

27/11/2016
David Cowlishaw@davidcowlishaw

I LOVE @MameDiouf99

27/11/2016
Espleypotter@Marcespley

After the worst start of a season for god knows how long, and we are still only 3 points behind ManU

28/11/2016
Dorset potter@cain_rosscain

3points behind last season and level with season before so we are doing ok 😂 😂 😂

02/12/2016
Will@IamWillSCFC

Butland's finished isn't he? Hope the FA's insurance company has some deep pockets. What a disaster

03/12/2016   **Stoke City (2) 2 Burnley (0) 0**

(Two amazing goals against a side who are traditionally rubbish away from home. Walters cracks one over the keeper and in off the far post, but the second is even better. Marc Muniesa starts the move from his own penalty area, beats 2 men, feeds it to Imbula-then-Shaqiri-then-Arnie who crosses into the penalty area for...hang on, what's Muniesa doing there! One brilliant finish later, and it's 2-0. He then almost gets sent off for a professional foul, but just about gets away it.)

Premier League position: 9th

Order on MotD: 7th out of 7

03/12/2016
David Cowlishaw@davidcowlishaw

We're definitely losing today and I don't know why.

03/12/2016
DUCK MAGAZINE@DUCKmagstoke

"Is this a library", sing Burnley fans. Like they've ever been in one.

03/12/2016
David Cowlishaw@davidcowlishaw

The warm reception Kightly got when he came on was, er, 'generous'

03/12/2016
Will@IamWillSCFC

Two cracking saves from Lee Grant again today. I might have a man crush brewing up!

03/12/2016
David Cowlishaw@davidcowlishaw

Bruno and Muni were fantastic today. I loved how boring that second half was.

03/12/2016
Trouserdog@TrouserdogSCFC

It's not very often that we win on autopilot. Usually we're left crapping ourselves right up to the 90th min. Very comfortable

03/12/2016
Rob Doolan@ChiefDelilah

Diouf has been a revelation at wing back. Bizarre, but brilliant.

03/12/2016
Espleypotter@Marcespley

Don't care what Diouf say about him being a Striker. He is a wing back and a decent one too

03/12/2016
The Oatcake Fanzine@oatcakescfc

Excellent from Stoke, full of imaginative, free-flowing football and two great goals. But that's enough about the first half. #SCFC

03/12/2016
Will@IamWillSCFC

If Martins Indi has suffered a fractured cheekbone, just remember that the best referee this country has to offer decided to play on

03/12/2016
DUCK MAGAZINE@DUCKmagstoke

We had a centre half beat two players, carry his run on and end up in the box to volley in after a flowing move. Why moan?

03/12/2016
Will@IamWillSCFC

Leonardo Di Caprio at the end of titanic #thingsleegrantcouldsave

03/12/2016
Espleypotter@Marcespley

I am struggling to think when the last time one of our centre backs scored a goal

03/12/2016
Martin Smith@SolarSmudge

Died a little bit after the interval but no complaints at all. Good solid win. Well played Stoke!

03/12/2016
DUCK MAGAZINE@DUCKmagstoke

The last thing many have seen going to bed is Marc Muniesa's smile. Massive baby boom on 2/9/2017

04/12/2016
The Oatcake Fanzine@oatcakescfc

So, when was the last time an #SCFC centre half scored a goal from a free flowing move and not a set piece? We're going for Smithy in 1974!

04/12/2016
DUCK MAGAZINE@DUCKmagstoke

Watching MOTD, Muni's goal is even more impressive as his run is followed by a red line. Didn't see that at the game.

05/12/2016
Will@IamWillSCFC

Wolves at home, will take that all day long. Go on Stoke!

10/12/2016   Arsenal (1) 3 Stoke City (1) 1

(No surprises here. Stoke lose at The Emirates again. It's their 15th consecutive defeat at Arsenal since The Jam broke up (1982, OK?). Oh sure, other mediocre sides can get results there, and Adam even puts Stoke 1-0 up with a penalty. But then it's downhill all the way...oh just forget it...)

Premier League position: 11th

Order on MotD: 2nd out of 6

10/12/2016
David Cowlishaw@davidcowlishaw

Game over. Same old story. May as well forfeit this fixture.

10/12/2016
The Oatcake Fanzine@oatcakescfc

A decent performance from The Potters, but the usual Emirates outcome. Another week, another elbow to a Stoke player's head goes unpunished.

10/12/2016
David Cowlishaw@davidcowlishaw

Where's the fucking red card? Where's the tucking football on this telly Charlie Adam has scored Fuckiy shit hell fuck

---

11/12/2016
Terry Conroy@TerryConroy

The Islington branch of Specsavers will be busy Monday morning.First appointment is Mr A Wenger(again?)

13/12/2016
Will@IamWillSCFC

A club who's fans' repertoire includes "Ryan Shawcross, we wish you would die" There are no bigger hypocrites in football than these tools

14/12/2016   Stoke City 0 Southampton 0

(Arnie is red carded on 26 minutes, and it's all hands to the pumps for the rest of the game. Not much else to say about this home draw.)

Premier League position: 12th

Order on MotD: 8th out of 8

14/12/2016
Will@IamWillSCFC

Baffling decision to drop the 3 players he has, but in Hughes we trust. Go on Stoke!

14/12/2016
David Cowlishaw@davidcowlishaw

Who is 2016/17's Xherdan Shaqiri? I.e. famous player at a big club who'd be frustratingly inconsistent for Stoke?

14/12/2016
HAIRY POTTER@cosnakickbo

He's had a Beer, He's had a Curry, @Charlie26Adam He's in No Hurry !!!!!!!! #STOSOU

14/12/2016
David Cowlishaw@davidcowlishaw

Ah well, at least the bench is swimming with pace, youth and guile

---

14/12/2016
Espleypotter@Marcespley

.@stokecity played with a player less for 70 mins but Southampton only managed 1 more shot on target over the game #Solid

---

14/12/2016
DUCK MAGAZINE@DUCKmagstoke

Better than winning

15/12/2016
The Oatcake Fanzine@oatcakescfc

So, another game and another elbow on a Stoke City player goes unpunished.

15/12/2016
Will@IamWillSCFC

In the past 3 games, Stoke players have been on the end of 3 deliberate elbows. And the number of red cards for them? Zero! Pathetic @fa

16/12/2016
Trouserdog@TrouserdogSCFC

As much as I loved the guy pre-injury, Bojan is too ineffective too often these days. No sleep lost if we cash in.

17/12/2016   Stoke City (2) 2 Leicester (0) 2

(THIS home draw has a LOT to say about it, and will be talked about for years, mainly for all the wrong reasons. By half time Stoke are 2-0 up, and Leicester are down to 10 men with most of the rest on yellow cards. That's a long way to come downhill from, but a dreadful second half almost sees Stoke tumble all the way to the bottom. It's going to be a cold cold Christmas after this debacle)

Premier League position: 11th

Order on MotD: 2nd out of 6

17/12/2016
David Cowlishaw@davidcowlishaw

For probably the first and only time, I'll be really disappointed if we don't beat the Champions of England today.

17/12/2016
HAIRY POTTER@cosnakickbo

They're Here They're There They're Every F###### Where YELLOW CARDSSS ...... #STOLEI

17/12/2016
DUCK MAGAZINE@DUCKmagstoke

Fair play to Ranieri... In 15 mins he calmed a team who had lost the plot completely and were 2-0 down. Outstanding management.

17/12/2016
Will@IamWillSCFC

How can people question Vardy's red? It's the very definition of "out of control"

17/12/2016
David Cowlishaw@davidcowlishaw

It was a red card, a penalty and all the bookings were fair. Leicester fans were great value in their indignation though so fair play.

17/12/2016
DUCK MAGAZINE@DUCKmagstoke

Only Stoke can **** this up

17/12/2016
Dave@davematthews79

I'm still fuming! All they had to do was hang on and I'd have won £250 on my accumulator. Useless bastards the lot of them

17/12/2016
The Oatcake Fanzine@oatcakescfc

A truly embarrassing half from players and management alike. Our Inability to see games out is amateurish. Pathetic.

17/12/2016
DUCK MAGAZINE@DUCKmagstoke

Hughes got the first half spot on. Which makes the second unfathomable. Totally distraught. As bad a 45 minutes as we've had in years

17/12/2016
Dorset potter@cain_rosscain

I like sparky but that was a textbook example of a manager panicking and chucking away 2 points saw him with my own eyes fear 😨

17/12/2016
Dave@davematthews79

Pathetic amateurish dross second half. Hughes tactically inept, where were the subs we needed? Embarrassing. I hate football.

17/12/2016
Martin Smith@SolarSmudge

So desperately sorry to say but Mark Hughes' worst day as Stoke manager. Shocking approach to second half (again!) No attempt to play!

17/12/2016
David Cowlishaw@davidcowlishaw

From about February, Hughes has picked his team based on players' tweets, transfer rumours and age. The man's a doddering fool.

17/12/2016
Rob Doolan@ChiefDelilah

The manager has to carry the can for that. Took the result for granted and completely failed to react to their changes.

17/12/2016
Neil Finney@NeilFinney

Even by Stokes ability to chuck games away that's pretty impressive #scfc

17/12/2016
DUCK MAGAZINE@DUCKmagstoke

Ruining weekends, since 1863

17/12/2016
David Cowlishaw@davidcowlishaw

Be sound when we beat a poor Watford at home and we won't be allowed to criticise Hughes again.

19/12/2016
Will@IamWillSCFC

Two biggest myths being banded on twitter: Jet fuel can't melt steel beams and being pushed makes you jump two footed into a challenge

19/12/2016
David Lee@stoke_city_pub

Last word on #scfc v #LCFC Definitely a red card, definitely a penalty, @MameDiouf99 man-of-the-match, @GaryLineker a nice guy but wrong ;-)

27/12/2016   Liverpool (2) 4 Stoke City (1) 1

(Stoke start with ex-Pool Crouch and Everton fan Walters, and sparkle for 30 minutes. Walters even scores! But it's all downhill from there... etc etc)

Premier League position: 13th

Order on MotD: (N/A)

27/12/2016
David Cowlishaw@davidcowlishaw

Two misplaced simple balls from Whelan in the first five minutes. Gonna be one of those games.

27/12/2016
David Lee@stoke_city_pub

An away side (Stoke) has taken the lead at Anfield in the Prem for first time since May (Chelsea).

27/12/2016
David Cowlishaw@davidcowlishaw

ERIK PIETERS CROSSED THE BALL

27/12/2016
Rob Doolan@ChiefDelilah

Is it worrying that our 'vote for Stoke as City of Culture!' logo looks like the Death Star?

27/12/2016
David Cowlishaw@davidcowlishaw

Wish Sky would start gushing over Liverpool when they go 4-1 up.

27/12/2016
Rob Doolan@ChiefDelilah

This is turning into a pretty shit night.

27/12/2016
Dorset potter@cain_rosscain

Why does it have to be exactly like we thought

27/12/2016
Espleypotter@Marcespley

Shocking, we have gifted Liverpool 3 goals. Never has a side gave the ball away so much

27/12/2016
HAIRY POTTER@cosnakickbo

MH Change is Good Anytime after 60 mins Look Up The Definition of Substitutions #STOSOU #STOLEI #LIVSTO

27/12/2016
Espleypotter@Marcespley

66% passing success says it all

27/12/2016
David Cowlishaw@davidcowlishaw

The worst thing about that horrorshow is we're patting each other on the back for a decent first twenty minutes.

27/12/2016
Clive Bickley@Bickers1952

Well give them 4 goals they don't have to work for and thats what you get. Hard enough task without making it so easy for them.

27/12/2016
Will@IamWillSCFC

Missed your chance Hughes. Utter wank

27/12/2016
David Cowlishaw@davidcowlishaw

Worst Liverpool-based sub? 18% Yellow Submarine, 82% Mark Hughes in 5 minutes

27/12/2016
Danny Bowers@dannybowers10

@oatcakescfc Went 1-0 and fell apart to simple goals. Poor game management. Afellay looked really good on his return though, good positive.

27/12/2016
David Cowlishaw@davidcowlishaw

Imbula has had a shocker today. So have many. Game plan lasted 20 minutes and once again Hughes doesn't have a backup plan.

27/12/2016
DUCK MAGAZINE@DUCKmagstoke

Disagreeing with the manager is one thing, but the name calling isn't on

27/12/2016
The Oatcake Fanzine@oatcakescfc

Some long, hard thinking for our manager to do. Some of the goals we're conceding would embarrass Sunday League players. Not good enough.

27/12/2016
Dorset potter@cain_rosscain

Exactly same result as April haven't improved at all ps Liverpool good enough with out our help

27/12/2016
The Oatcake Fanzine@oatcakescfc

How have we got ourselves in a position where we're playing an away game at Anfield with no recognised defender on our bench?

29/12/2016
Rob Doolan@ChiefDelilah

I think we're looking forward far more than we did under the old regime. We have ambitions, we're just getting stuff wrong.

27/12/2016
DUCK MAGAZINE@DUCKmagstoke

Wolves is a massive, massive game. Club needs a cup run.

27/12/2016
Rob Doolan@ChiefDelilah

Don't want to frighten you but there's a teensy possibility we won't get a result at Chelsea either.

27/12/2016
DUCK MAGAZINE@DUCKmagstoke

We'll not lose at Chelsea. There, I said it.

26/12/2016
The Oatcake Fanzine@oatcakescfc

Congratulations to Chelsea on their club record 12th straight win. Next up though, the Mighty Potters. #unlucklythirteen

31/12/2016   Chelsea (1) 4 Stoke City (0) 2

(Why do Stoke keep conceding 4 goals??! Well, a New Year's Eve game against Chelsea who've won their previous 12 Premier games, was always going to end this way. On the plus side? Chelsea have only conceded 4 goals at home all season, so Stoke's two goals looks quite impressive...doesn't it...?)

Premier League position: 14th

Order on MotD: 1st out of 8

31/12/2016
Trouserdog@TrouserdogSCFC

Confident about this afternoon- confident I'm going to eat dinner, then have a poo, then start drinking- forget Chelsea, we'll get dicked

---

31/12/2016
Dorset potter@cain_rosscain

Sparky seems to pick teams the same way Bowie used to write songs drop random names on a table mix them up hey presto

---

31/12/2016
Trouserdog@TrouserdogSCFC

Right, I'm having a Stoke following frenzy...if you're a Stoke fan you're getting followed (only on here, not to your home) #SCFC

31/12/2016
Will@IamWillSCFC

Even I'm struggling to find anything positive about that line up.

31/12/2016
Trouserdog@TrouserdogSCFC

Fucking hell. Our defence is looser than yer Grandma's bowels. :-(

31/12/2016
HAIRY POTTER@cosnakickbo

BRUNO MARTINS INDI GOALLLLLLLLL 2016 1-1 1st Attempt 100% Success Rate Shots on Target #stokecity

31/12/2016
Rob Doolan@ChiefDelilah

BRUNO MARTINS INDI...MARTINS INDI OOOOOOOOOH

31/12/2016
Trouserdog@TrouserdogSCFC

Does Adam actually know what colour we're playing in?

31/12/2016
Will@IamWillSCFC

9 defenders v Gary Cahill. Cahill wins the header! Utter toss that is Stoke!

31/12/2016
Trouserdog@TrouserdogSCFC

'It's a shock to see Stoke concede from a set piece" OTHER SHOCK NEWS: bear shits in woods.

31/12/2016
The Oatcake Fanzine@oatcakescfc

A decent effort from Stoke, but the third goal killed us. Our game management is poor beyond belief. Some big, big games coming up now.

31/12/2016
David Lee@stoke_city_pub

Stoke City lost 8 games conceding 4+ goals in a calendar year (2016) for 1st time since 1952. 1st time it's EVER happened in Premier League

31/12/2016
Trouserdog@TrouserdogSCFC

Good fucking riddance 2016.

31/12/2016
DUCK MAGAZINE@DUCKmagstoke

Thank god that bone idle Arnautovic missed the last three games, eh?

31/12/2016
David Lee@stoke_city_pub

Only ONE other Premier League side conceded more goals than Stoke City in 2016! #scfc defence is a problem.

31/12/2016
Clive Bickley@Bickers1952

When are we going to start doing to teams what they find so easy to do to us?

31/12/2016
Dorset potter@cain_rosscain

At least we didn't embarrass ourselves like we did against Liverpool

01/01/2017
David Lee@stoke_city_pub

Stoke City have conceded 68 league goals in 2016, 66% more than 2015!!! 66%!!! #scfc

02/01/2017
Trouserdog@TrouserdogSCFC

We've been truly shafted with Xmas fixtures this year. No Boxing Day game, no New Year's Day game...I've had to spend time with the wife FFS

Stoke City (1) 2 Watford (0) 0

(Stoke complete their first double of the season, faster than any other club in the Prem (er, apart from Man City), and it's only January 3rd! Scruffy goals either side of half-time...well, they all count. Nothing to write home about, but try stopping these guys doing so anyway:)

Premier League position: 11th

Order on MotD: N/A

03/01/2017
Neil Finney@NeilFinney

A 6 pointer tonight then eh? Just 3 will do, with a couple of goals and no ref calamities. Too much to ask? #STKWAT #scfc

---

03/01/2017
DUCK MAGAZINE@DUCKmagstoke

Its not so much the composition of the team, but the set up. Big fan of 4-2-3-1 with Arnie left.

03/01/2017
Espleypotter@Marcespley

I agree their is a time & a place for this team selection. Against a shit Watford side at home ain't one of them

---

03/01/2017
The Oatcake Fanzine@oatcakescfc

Talking to a Stokie over from Oz for his first game in five years. Last time he saw us Crouch and Walters led the line. He's in for a shock!

03/01/2017
Dorset potter@cain_rosscain

He does realise he's playing a team full of injurys and hardly any confidence at home dosnt he ??

03/01/2017
Neil Finney@NeilFinney

Imagine having Xherdan Shaqiri in your team and leaving him on the bench.

03/01/2017
Espleypotter@Marcespley

What a fantastic 5 a side team you could make from Stoke's BENCH

03/01/2017
Will@IamWillSCFC

Imagine your club captain scoring and then cupping his hands to his ears towards his fans

03/01/2017
David Cowlishaw@davidcowlishaw

Best moment of a shockingly awful first half: Arnie plucking a wayward ball out the air on his toe. I go to football for those moments.

03/01/2017
Will@IamWillSCFC

This is a team playing with absolutely zero confidence. It's been sucked out of them by shit team selection after shit team selection

03/01/2017
Trouserdog@TrouserdogSCFC

I can never remember whether it's double 'f' or double 'l', but tbh, Afellay/Affelay transcends letters. He's a slinky Dutch sex machine

03/01/2017
Will@IamWillSCFC

Shawcross needlessly concedes a free kick in a dangerous position. Stoke fans all cup their ears in his direction

03/01/2017
Trouserdog@TrouserdogSCFC

Crouch is playing...WAAAA! Walters is playing....WAAA! Adam is playing....WAA! Hughes out....WAAA! Oh look we've won 2-0.

03/01/2017
Espleypotter@Marcespley

No Stoke player eligible to play for England had scored for 56 games prior to Crouch v Chelsea, now Shawcross gets in on the act

03/01/2017
DUCK MAGAZINE@DUCKmagstoke

Two good crosses Two goals Rocket science

03/01/2017
Rob Doolan@ChiefDelilah

To play this badly and be winning to nil almost feels like some sort of bizarre performance art.

03/01/2017
Espleypotter@Marcespley

Adam MOM, who was match sponsor, Wrights pies?

03/01/2017
Neil Finney@NeilFinney

Much needed win for Stoke tonight. Awful game, freezing cold, but best laugh at the footie in ages 😁 #scfc

03/01/2017

Espleypotter@Marcespley

What's everyone moaning at, we are unbeaten this year what more can they do 😃

03/01/2017

Dorset potter@cain_rosscain

Lads lads this is the game you were supposed to show us that everything is fine no need to worry not pass the prosac

04/01/2017

David Lee@stoke_city_pub

Sparky got it right, played a side to deal with very physical Watford. Walters/Adam for Bojan/Shaq. Not pretty, but impressive

04/01/2017

David Cowlishaw@davidcowlishaw

sunshine and happiness from today Joe Allen was good Solid pint of Pedigree M6 not that bad Everything @NOLAStokie does

04/01/2017

Trouserdog@TrouserdogSCFC

Why all the tampons being yanked out over team selection? MH picked a team...it won. There's nothing more that he can do than that.

07/01/2017   Stoke City (0) 0 Wolves (1) 2

(Stoke's first-team lose easily at home in the cup to a seriously-understrength gold-shirted brace-scoring side ...hang on, haven't we had this one before?!? No, that was the Hull cup defeat, this is the Wolves cup defeat. The only argument amongst Stoke fans surely is whether this is worse than the Leicester debacle?)

07/01/2017
David Cowlishaw@davidcowlishaw

I bloody love the FA Cup. Just win @stokecity

06/01/2017
David Lee@stoke_city_pub

Mark Hughes' 1st league win as Fulham mgr was against Wolves. Bobby Zamora broke leg, Berra sent off, & Fulham win 2-1 with 91min free kick

---

07/01/2017
HAIRY POTTER@cosnakickbo

We've Got Our Name on The Cup 🍀🍀🍀🍀 #EmiratesFACup #STKWOL #STOWOL

07/01/2017
Dorset potter@cain_rosscain

Can't Moan about the line up today over to you lads make us proud again 😌😌

07/01/2017
Neil Finney@NeilFinney

Do all visiting goalies save there best for us. Not once have I seen one have a shocker...never.

07/01/2017
Will@IamWillSCFC

Say what you like about Whelan/Walters technically, but when neither are on the pitch there is zero leadership, ZERO

07/01/2017
DUCK MAGAZINE@DUCKmagstoke

The whole season's on the line here lads, in a game against hated rivals, and we are miles off the pace.

07/01/2017
Neil Finney@NeilFinney

I thought Hughes had subbed the entire team for Joe Allen when he came out on his own 2nd half...might have worked.

07/01/2017
Danny Bowers@dannybowers10

If only we could sub our entire 11,its the fa cup and none of players have fight in a local derby. It's embarrassing.

07/01/2017
Neil Finney@NeilFinney

Particularly enjoyed the chat with the Wolves fans before the game who told us that was there reserve team and we'd be fine. Cheers

07/01/2017
Dave@davematthews79

we have been so awful first half. I think our team think they just have to turn up to beat "lowly" Wolves. Disgraceful.

07/01/2017
DUCK MAGAZINE@DUCKmagstoke

45 minutes of the season left?

07/01/2017
Neil Finney@NeilFinney

What was that at the end Arnie...giving your boots to a fan? Are you retiring?

07/01/2017
Will@IamWillSCFC

Did our club captain cup his ears again as he trudged off the pitch?

07/01/2017
Danny Bowers@dannybowers10

Don't get me started on Shawcross either, the guys been awful for months and my dog could be a better captain. Shocking.

07/01/2017
Neil Finney@NeilFinney

So #dryjanuary lasted until today, well done Stoke, well done. Cheers 🍺

07/01/2017
DUCK MAGAZINE@DUCKmagstoke

And people want us to draw Vale in a cup???!!!!!

07/01/2017
Neil Finney@NeilFinney

Usually I can drag a positive or two out of a defeat. Today...nothing.

07/01/2017
Martin Smith@SolarSmudge

That was a great FA Cup tie for 30 minutes in the 2nd half. For the rest of the game though that was dreadful from Stoke!

07/01/2017
Neil Finney@NeilFinney

Another glorious cup run comes to an end #scfc

07/01/2017
David Lee@stoke_city_pub

Just when you think you've seen the worst Stoke performance for years, a worse one comes along to eclipse it. #dire #putrid

07/01/2017
Rob Doolan@ChiefDelilah

There's no more defending Hughes now. We're seeing the last days of his reign just as we were Pulis' four years ago.

07/01/2017
Espleypotter@Marcespley

Throughly disappointing display. We needed to show fight and pace and showed neither.

07/01/2017
Danny Bowers@dannybowers10

No Stoke player deserves credit today, you've all been shocking and offered no fight or commitment. Our season is over, thanks lads.

07/01/2017
DUCK MAGAZINE@DUCKmagstoke

Stoke City Making pissed off folk go shopping in late January since 1863

08/01/2017
The Oatcake Fanzine@oatcakescfc

No excuses for yesterday's defeat, but this is a penalty all day long.

08/01/2017
Will@IamWillSCFC

Been following Stoke for 31 years and for the first time I'm falling out of love with them. This squad and their attitude is unrecognisable

08/01/2017
Clive Bickley@Bickers1952

No excuse for our performance but definitely a penalty. Changes the whole complex of the game if given.

08/01/2017
Dorset potter@cain_rosscain

Feel let down by Bojan the fans including me have stuck with him through thick and thin trouble is it's all thin at moment

09/01/2017
David Lee@stoke_city_pub

Martin Spinks: "Mark Hughes, a man clearly feeling somewhat betrayed by his highly-paid flair players" #sentinel

09/01/2017
Will@IamWillSCFC

Peter Crouch has scored 49 goals for this club. Can we stop changing history and pretending he's been useless?

09/01/2017
David Lee@stoke_city_pub

Sparky a "victim of his own success"? I think not. He's a victim of Chairman Coates' reasoning for his appointment back in 2013, methinks.

09/01/2017
Espleypotter@Marcespley

Mike Dean is ref v Sunderland, what could possible go wrong

09/01/2017
Espleypotter@Marcespley

Might as well not play Shawcross Saturday,as Mr Look-at-me will be looking for every reason to pull him up. #RedCardAlert #AllAboutHim #Dean

10/01/2017
David Lee@stoke_city_pub

Coates explicitly brought him in to be better for results, style of play, & not to waste money on big money signings. Ooops!

11/01/2017
The Oatcake Fanzine@oatcakescfc

Why is Mame getting so much stick for his open goal miss? Anyone would think he's our centre forward.

12/01/2017
Will@IamWillSCFC

For the first time in forever I'm contemplating whether to renew or not next season. Disillusioned isn't the word

14/01/2017   Sunderland (1) 1 Stoke City (3) 3

(These doubles are turning up thick and fast as David Moyes' flaky Black Cats are swept aside in the first half-hour. Crouch now on 99 Premier League goals. Oh, the excitement!)

Premier League position: 9th

Order on MotD: 6th out of 8

14/01/2017
Neil Finney@NeilFinney

#Matchday Sunderland away, not going...bound to win. Off to the @ UK_PCS

14/01/2017
David Cowlishaw@davidcowlishaw

Shaq and Arnie today. Against mediocre sides they only need perform for half an hour tops. Incredible that they're stoke players.

14/01/2017
Trouserdog@TrouserdogSCFC

I gave Shaq loads of stick last week- only fair to give him praise this week. Best display for ages; looked quality.

14/01/2017
Will@IamWillSCFC

it's only my 2nd win in 12 games this season. Was beginning to think I was the problem!

14/01/2017
David Cowlishaw@davidcowlishaw

Yeah, my Hughes doubts are the same. But he got it right today and it was a much needed win. An absolutely ace day.

14/01/2017
Will@IamWillSCFC

Excellent win today, much more like it Stoke! No complaints from me tonight

14/01/2017
Trouserdog@TrouserdogSCFC

If MOTD don't dedicate the entire show to our second goal then I'm writing a strongly worded letter to @GaryLineker and John Logie-Baird

14/01/2017
The Oatcake Fanzine@oatcakescfc

So you're not going to talk about one of the best Premier League goals of the season @BBCMOTD ? Truly pathetic. You're dead to us.

14/01/2017
Espleypotter@Marcespley

Just saying if @Arsenal had scored Arnautovic's second goal, twitter would not here the end of it from their supporters

15/01/2017
Espleypotter@Marcespley

Those that criticise Shaqiri for being inconsistent need to realise that if he was consistant, then he would not be at Stoke Full stop

15/01/2017
Clive Bickley@Bickers1952

Will the real SCFC turn up please or were Sunderland just worse than Wolves 2nd XI? When Arnie and Shaq perform we do as a team

21/01/2017   **Stoke City (1) 1 Man Utd (0) 1**

(The late-late-late-late equaliser for Wayne Rooney, as he breaks United's scoring record, is all anyone wants to hear about in the media. So, nobody wants to know about Stoke being unbeaten by United in a season & their heartbreak at the end of this game. It's not fair!!)

Premier League position: 9th

Order on MotD: 3rd out of 7

21/01/2017
DUCK MAGAZINE@DUCKmagstoke

See United have Clatto in the starting line up

21/01/2017
Will@IamWillSCFC

Looking forward to a rendition of "Ibrahimovic, your nose is offside" amongst others today

---

21/01/2017
DUCK MAGAZINE@DUCKmagstoke

Half time at the bet365, and Stoke have a one goal lead in this battle to see who wins the midtable this season

---

21/01/2017
David Cowlishaw@davidcowlishaw

Whelan superb. Great collective display too. Sickener but it feels like Stoke are back at the moment. Oh and Ngoy needs more minutes.

21/01/2017
The Oatcake Fanzine@oatcakescfc

A sickening time to lose the lead but we can't complain. That was a great effort from the team though we rode our luck at times #scfcvsmufc

21/01/2017
Will@IamWillSCFC

Statues have been erected for less than Whelan produced on that pitch this afternoon

21/01/2017
Espleypotter@Marcespley

Gutted with the result, defended as well as we did v Southampton. ManU pressed us well but we did have a couple of decent breaks Take a draw

21/01/2017
Terry Conroy@TerryConroy

A great "Team" effort today.With all the Utd stars on view ,rarely did they get in behind us or open us up.it shows our true capabilities.

21/01/2017
DUCK MAGAZINE@DUCKmagstoke

In celebration of his goalscoring record, Wayne Rooney is washing his hair. It's currently on fast spin.

(Finally, after literally years of clandestine meetings, off/on negotiations, and pure desperation Saido Berahino signs for £12m???! Bargain.)

03/12/2016
DUCK MAGAZINE@DUCKmagstoke

To the rest of the football world: Bruno Martins Indi is crap. Pass it on.

03/12/2016
Dorset potter@cain_rosscain

Lee Grant Jan is decision time do you want to go back to Derby under that weapons grade bell end McLaren or stay with the mighty potters ??

16/12/2016
Will@IamWillSCFC

Are we really going to turn down Lee Grant over £4 million? They're taking the piss but we have no option.

16/12/2016
Will@IamWillSCFC

Hughes won't be held to ransom? We have no other choice. Numerous other clubs world take him at £4 million given his recent form I'm sure

---

01/01/2017
Trouserdog@TrouserdogSCFC

Come on Hughes, why haven't you signed anyone yet? Pull your fucking finger out.

05/01/2017
David Cowlishaw@davidcowlishaw

Hughes obviously really rates Berahino. Dread to think what happens if he signs him and it doesn't work out.

05/01/2017
Will@IamWillSCFC

It's crazy going after Berahino when we already have Johnson and Bardsley who can play right back!

05/01/2017
David Cowlishaw@davidcowlishaw

A new contract for 35-year-old Peter Crouch. Until recently a 3rd/4th choice striker. Bojan, our only true no. 10, gets shipped out. TP2.

06/01/2017
Will@IamWillSCFC

Bojan leaving will be this generations Matthews/Greenhoff. The fans won't forgive this, some will never return

07/01/2017
Trouserdog@TrouserdogSCFC

Shaq £12m, Bojan £8m, Imbula 50p and a Twix bar. None of them are playing like they want to be here. Get them gone and move on.

09/01/2017
Espleypotter@Marcespley

If Mark Hughes says that Bojan is still in his plans then he won't be sold. We don't need to,his contract is long enough for us not to worry

16/01/2017
David Cowlishaw@davidcowlishaw

Bojan is so obviously gonna score against us for Middlesbrough I may as well just put a grand on it now.

20/01/2017
Will@IamWillSCFC

Just imagine the tribunal in the Summer for a fat bloke who hasn't played for 2 years. West Brom are playing a very dangerous game here

20/01/2017
Neil Finney@NeilFinney

The face on Pulis when Saido bags the winner against West Brom. Get it done Stoke, worth every penny.

20/01/2017
David Cowlishaw@davidcowlishaw

Saido Berahino to the tune of Hi ho silver lining would be a step up from our usual

24/01/2017
Espleypotter@Marcespley

Would Charlie Adam fancy Turkey, of course he would. Especially with roast potatoes and three veg

29/01/2017
The Oatcake Fanzine@oatcakescfc

Sad to see Bojan leaving for Mainz. Truly hope this isn't the end for him at Stoke.

31/01/2017
Espleypotter@Marcespley

Imbula leaving is gossip as far as I can make out

01/02/2017   Stoke City (1) 1 Everton (1) 1

(Crouch does The Robot goal-celebration after scoring his 100th Premier goal on 7 minutes! Worth the admission price alone. But in one of the most surreal moments in modern football, the ref unwisely overrules the linesman's offside flag, after being savagely mobbed by Everton players, and awards them a goal. Despite the final touch from intercepting Shawcross, Lukaku is clearly offside and interfering with our Ryan! Everyone rushes over to get their rule book out.)

Premier League position: 9th

Order on MotD: N/A

01/02/2017
Will@IamWillSCFC

He's offside surely?! If he's not there, Shawcross doesn't need to swing at it. Horse shit decision

---

01/02/2017
Espleypotter@Marcespley

If Shawcross leaves it Lakaku scores & would of been ruled offside,why because Ryan has to intervene 2 stop Lakaku does it not mean the same

---

01/02/2017
HAIRY POTTER@cosnakickbo

Lay Grent, Jon Sun, Brew Know, Sindy, Show Croz, Payters, Wheel Un, Add Um, R Knee, Hal Hun, Crow Chee, R Phil Lie, Shack Ear Ree, Bars Lee
☕🍺👍

02/02/2017
The Oatcake Fanzine@oatcakescfc

So when was this rule abolished then? "Running to contest decisions, arguing face-to-face with officials & visible disrespectful actions will result in yellow cards"

02/02/2017
Terry Conroy@TerryConroy

So many good performances last night v Everton.MOM could have been any one.Consistency will get us a top 8 place.?!!

04/02/2017   West Brom (1) 1 Stoke City (0) 0

(As predictable as the seasons, Tony Pulis beats his former club again with an early goal. Berahino comes on as sub against his old side to a hostile reaction. Pulis and Sparky fail to shake hands, and each rightly blames the other. Pantomime at its very best!)

Premier League position: 11th

Order on MotD: 8th out of 8

04/02/2017
Neil Finney@NeilFinney

So TP doesn't "give a damn" about Saidos future eh? Classy that Tony. He's lost a top player and he knows it. #scfc

---

04/02/2017
Dorset potter@cain_rosscain

F F S lads remember Pulis is going to try and get a few of you sent off don't fall for it please

---

04/02/2017
Rob Doolan@ChiefDelilah

Is there a slower team than us in thought or deed in the league?

04/02/2017
David Cowlishaw@davidcowlishaw

Ah well, we had loads of British lads playing so I assume we showed heart and desire, right?

04/02/2017
Rob Doolan@ChiefDelilah

Stoke pay the price for a hideous first half in which they suffered the embarrassment of being completely outplayed by a Pulis team.

04/02/2017
Neil Finney@NeilFinney

persistently over passing the ball. Trying to walk it in. Frustrating.

04/02/2017
The Oatcake Fanzine@oatcakescfc

Absolutely abysmal. All huff and puff with no end product.

04/02/2017
Neil Finney@NeilFinney

Predictably Pulis that #binary

04/02/2017
David Cowlishaw@davidcowlishaw

We had an identity under Pulis, but grew weary of it. Hughes started to develop a new identity, got weary of it before we did, and now?

04/02/2017
Espleypotter@Marcespley

Got up for work at 02:00 and it was pretty cold. Feel for those sleeping in the concourse at the bet365 raising money for the homeless

05/02/2017
David Lee@stoke_city_pub

The last (& only) time Stoke City have beaten a Tony Pulis side is when Neil Baldwin dressed as a chicken in the Scfc dug-out. Simples

11/02/2017
Trouserdog@TrouserdogSCFC

TBH I couldn't care less if TP had left messages on Ryan's phone asking him what knickers he was wearing. The man is ancient history now.

11/02/2017　　　　Stoke City (0) 1 Crystal Palace (0) 0

(At last, Palace are tamed after a run of 5 humiliating defeats to them...yes, but that's enough of that. Big Sam Allardyce returns to the bet365, but for some reason is no longer manager of England. Brilliant Young Egyptian Ramadan Sobhi makes his first home start, only to find Arnie wants to play on the left wing too. Embarrassing! So they take it in turns, and between them they combine to create the only goal for Joe Allen. If only all matters can be solved so easily.)

Premier League position: 9th

Order on MotD: 6th out of 7

10/02/2017
David Lee@stoke_city_pub

Stoke City (& Sparky) have lost 6 out of the last 7 games to Crystal Palace, with 1 draw. A win will be a major achievement.

11/02/2017
Will@IamWillSCFC

Palace chairman overtook me on the M6 in his Ferrari whilst texting, absolute throbber

---

11/02/2017
Dorset potter@cain_rosscain

According to the programme Joe Allen is a fan of Metallica . Enter sandman is a great track to get the dressing room buzzing

---

11/02/2017
Trouserdog@TrouserdogSCFC

So cold today I took-and used-a blanket. Back at The Vic I'd have been forcibly ejected from the terrace and sent to The Boothen Stand

---

11/02/2017
David Cowlishaw@davidcowlishaw

Bruno good, Ramadan good, Afellay good. Absolutely fucking crying out for a Bojan or Imbula though.

11/02/2017
Will@IamWillSCFC

Stoke game was awful, fortunately Palace look doomed, they were dreadful

11/02/2017
DUCK MAGAZINE@DUCKmagstoke

3 points for Stoke = a great Saturday Always was, always is, and always will be. Anything else is conjecture.

11/02/2017
Rob Doolan@ChiefDelilah

Am I the only person who thought we played pretty well today?

11/02/2017
DUCK MAGAZINE@DUCKmagstoke

Affelay been superb Bruno MOTM

11/02/2017
David Cowlishaw@davidcowlishaw

Whelan's defiant "Fuck off" of the ball into the stands really encapsulated the spirit of the match.

11/02/2017
Rob Doolan@ChiefDelilah

Professional performance from Stoke - deserved to win and rarely looked in danger after scoring. Goal was quality from start to finish.

11/02/2017
DUCK MAGAZINE@DUCKmagstoke

Atkinson reffed that superbly today

11/02/2017
David Cowlishaw@davidcowlishaw

Can't pretend that was anything other than a diabolical game. Result obviously most important thing but then why did we sack TP?

11/02/2017
Rob Doolan@ChiefDelilah

The team looks much better balanced with Sobhi in it.

11/02/2017
The Oatcake Fanzine@oatcakescfc

The silliness ends! Lovely three points and a wonderful goal to win the game. Class from Arnie and Ramadan and a great finish from Joe.

11/02/2017
Will@IamWillSCFC

Sobhi was mesmerising today at times, looks a right player. And Bruno might just be the greatest bloke to ever walk this earth #colossus

11/02/2017
Espleypotter@Marcespley

Been awake since 02:00 this morning, only not snoring due to the adrenaline from a Stoke win and due to still thawing out from the game

11/02/2017
Dorset potter@cain_rosscain

Not pretty today but so what very pretty goal 3 points our defence is back had chat with hairy potter cracking day now for some

11/02/2017
Martin Smith@SolarSmudge

Perfectly happy with that today, against a bogey team. Special shout-outs to Whelan, Shawcross and Martins Indi! #scfc

11/02/2017
David Cowlishaw@davidcowlishaw

Spotted: Match of the Day producers trying to pay Channel Five to put our game on the football league show.

12/02/2017
Terry Conroy@TerryConroy

Anybody watching my interview in The Waddington Suite after the game yesterday with Arnie,couldn't fail to be impressed with his belief.!

17/02/2017
Dave@davematthews79

Great news that @stokecity season ticket prizes have been frozen for the 10th consecutive year! I love my club! #DEVOT10N

23/02/2017
Neil Finney@NeilFinney

Rainieri sacked...Pulis checks phone.

24/02/2017
Will@IamWillSCFC

In work at the weekend to pay for my season ticket next week. Haven't begrudged it so much since Pulis' last season

26/02/2017   Spurs (4) 4 Stoke City (0) 0

(In yet ANOTHER 0-4 dicking by Spurs, at least Stoke don't have a disallowed goal and Sparky sent to the stands in search of wifi signal. What luck! Instead, Stoke concede early...and it's downhill all the way etc...well, to half time anyway. As it's now 0-4, Mark Hughes allegedly gives them a piece of his mind in the form of a ""hair-dryer"", and they put on an adequate 2nd half showing. If only Crouch had equalised early in the game...er, would it really have made any difference?)

Premier League position: 10th

Order on MotD: 2nd out of 3

27/02/2017
Will@IamWillSCFC

"It's 2017 and Stoke City are still lining up with Whelan, Adam and Crouch..."

24/02/2017
David Lee@stoke_city_pub

Mark Hughes ponders the contrast in game preparation between Spurs' 3 cup games & Stoke's Dubai trip.

26/02/2017
David Cowlishaw@davidcowlishaw

Ah, football. You dickhead.

27/02/2017
Will@IamWillSCFC

Can anyone tell me what our identity is under Hughes? Hard working, Defensively sound, physical, pacey, attacking, no, no, no, no and no

---

26/02/2017
Trouserdog@TrouserdogSCFC

45 minutes and it'll all be over. I think I'll stay on here for moral support.

27/02/2017
Will@IamWillSCFC

"'In this world nothing can be said to be certain, except death, taxes and Spurs 4 Stoke 0" Benjamin Franklin (1817)

26/02/2017
Trouserdog@TrouserdogSCFC

Good job Spurs are tired.

26/02/2017
Rob Doolan@ChiefDelilah

Go home Ryan Shawcross. You're drunk.

26/02/2017
Espleypotter@Marcespley

Get Cameron on, and while you are at it get Saido on too

26/02/2017
Rob Doolan@ChiefDelilah

You know that lad who scores all the goals? Yeah? Definitely don't mark him. It's the last thing they'll be expecting...

26/02/2017
Rob Doolan@ChiefDelilah

Also, setting up to play on the break with Peter Crouch on his own up front hasn't worked for SIX FUCKING YEARS.

26/02/2017
David Lee@stoke_city_pub

Just in case u haven't heard, I can watch today's Stoke match free on Sky channel 407. It's half time & (unsurprisingly) City are 0-4 down.

26/02/2017
The Oatcake Fanzine@oatcakescfc

Thanks to Spurs for declaring at half time. A pitiful performance from Stoke with only Sobhi, Grant and our great fans emerging with credit.

26/02/2017
Will@IamWillSCFC

We have zero pace zero identity and too many big name players who just don't turn up. This season has been utter dog shit, apathetic at best

26/02/2017
David Lee@stoke_city_pub

All credit to the Sky guys at the pre-match #scfc press conference who pressed Sparky about 0-4 defeats to Spurs. #Ididntseeitcoming

26/02/2017
Dorset potter@cain_rosscain

If you want to fill the new sized stadium it ain't going to happen with performances like that

26/02/2017
David Lee@stoke_city_pub

Despite losing 0-4, Sparky immediately & sportingly makes to shake hands with Spurs' manager…something he didn't do at WBA…

26/02/2017
Espleypotter@Marcespley

One positive from the game, we have not got to play Spurs this season again

26/02/2017
HAIRY POTTER@cosnakickbo

GMT 4 Past STOKE #DejaVu glad he didn't score as well

26/02/2017
DUCK MAGAZINE@DUCKmagstoke

Spurs totally disresecting the Premier League by resting their defence today

26/02/2017
Dorset potter@cain_rosscain

Dear sky stop putting us on TV sick of us getting our arses out infront of millions of football fans 😵 😵

27/02/2017
David Cowlishaw@davidcowlishaw

Wish I'd criticised Adam more on the pod tbh

27/02/2017
Will@IamWillSCFC

I think you get to a stage in your life where your heroes are no longer footballers or actors, they're your family, friends and colleagues

03/03/2017
Espleypotter@Marcespley

Shaqiri affects how we play, him missing is key to how much time Arnautovic gets on the ball.

04/03/2017   Stoke City (2) 2 Middlesbrough (0) 0

(It's really hotting up in the competition between Ramadan & Arnie. Arnie scores the goals, but Ramadan wows the crowd. The Austrian and the Egyptian; the odd couple.)

Premier League position: 9th

Order on MotD: 7th out of 8

04/03/2017
Espleypotter@Marcespley

Hopefully I can watch Stoke today without freezing my tits off

---

04/03/2017
David Cowlishaw@davidcowlishaw

Today isn't a must-win, but if we don't win we won't win again until April 15.

04/03/2017
Will@IamWillSCFC

We're playing 2 defensive midfielders at home against a team who currently sit 17th in the league. Absolutely wank Hughes!

04/03/2017
David Cowlishaw@davidcowlishaw

AND HE TRACKS BACK Ramadan is life

04/03/2017
Danny Bowers@dannybowers10

Well @RamadanSobhi is one of the best wingers I've seen down Stoke, what an incredible talent.

04/03/2017
Will@IamWillSCFC

Any danger of Arnautovic turning up this week?

05/03/2017
Espleypotter@Marcespley

Big shout out to the woman sat behind me who was giving Arnie stick from kick off, right upto the point he scored. He shut her right up

04/03/2017
David Cowlishaw@davidcowlishaw

Stoke won. I thought we were going down? :-)

04/03/2017
Rob Doolan@ChiefDelilah

Boro have been diabolical. Was expecting a reaction from them but they look like they're sleepwalking to relegation.

04/03/2017
Trouserdog@TrouserdogSCFC

Never seen a player deserve a goal more than Ramadan today. Brilliant from start to finish. Ramadan der-der-der-der-der

04/03/2017
Rob Doolan@ChiefDelilah

Surprised to see Whelan getting stick. Nobody completed more passes, nobody created more chances, in the top 5 for tackles and interceptions

04/03/2017
David Cowlishaw@davidcowlishaw

Today was ace. Still think we've had a underwhelming season and Hughes has made a bucketload of mistakes.

04/03/2017
Rob Doolan@ChiefDelilah

What a player Sobhi looks already. Shouldered the creative burden alone since Arnie went off and frightened the life out of them.

04/03/2017
The Oatcake Fanzine@oatcakescfc

Pity we couldn't add more goals but still a good win. Great first goal from Arnie and we have a new star in Ramadan. Hope Bruno's okay.

04/03/2017
Will@IamWillSCFC

Ramadan's performance today probably makes the top 10 individual performances since we've been promoted, that's how good it was

04/03/2017
Terry Conroy@TerryConroy

Three points never in doubt today.Great reception for all the Boys of 72.After all these years,they still love SCFC with so many memories

04/03/2017
Danny Bowers@dannybowers10

Good response from last week, @RamadanSobhi is an immense talent and the touch and finishing from Arnie today was quality.

04/03/2017
Dorset potter@cain_rosscain

Ramadan Sobhi is made my season seeing you play in our shirt

06/03/2017
David Lee@stoke_city_pub

Mark Hughes been at Stoke City for 3yrs 9m, his longest at any club. "I've another 2 yrs & I'd like to think I will get to the end of that"

08/03/2017   Manchester City 0 Stoke City 0

(Nope, dunno what happened here. Man City manage just ONE attempt on goal, AND - even more strangely - Stoke fail to fall apart and go downhill faster than an out-of-control gazelle. First team to keep clean sheet at Etihad this season.)

Premier League position: 9th

Order on MotD: N/A

08/03/2017
Dorset potter@cain_rosscain

Tonight a win is unlikely, a draw would be fantastic, a loose isn't the end of the world as long as we can leave heads held high .

08/03/2017
David Lee@stoke_city_pub

It has been noticed that Mark Hughes has been looking quite grey recently. I hope he's in ruder health than he looks…

08/03/2017
DUCK MAGAZINE@DUCKmagstoke

Dreadful team news for Stoke, with Stones not picked

08/03/2017
David Lee@stoke_city_pub

Pulis reckoned Saido Berahino was months away from match fitness to start a match. Sparky thought it would be weeks. Tonight we'll see

---

08/03/2017
Will@IamWillSCFC

Aguero trips over his own feet and Martin Tyler questions what colour card Shawcross is getting #modernfootballthat

---

08/03/2017
Rob Doolan@ChiefDelilah

Fair play to Sparky. That starting XI was David Icke level insane but it's done very well so far.

08/03/2017
David Cowlishaw@davidcowlishaw

Football is utterly magnificent. This opinion may change in the coming minutes.

08/03/2017
David Lee@stoke_city_pub

Is it fair to say that Kevin De Bruyne came out of that foul on a Stoke City player with a face looking like a smacked arse?! Yes.

08/03/2017
Espleypotter@Marcespley

Cameron once again the energy in Midfield along side Allen. Diouf tackles like a demon, Sobhi with the threat.Saido and Jon held ground well

08/03/2017
Rob Doolan@ChiefDelilah

Big beautiful bastard bore draw.

08/03/2017
Neil Finney@NeilFinney

Some good possession for Stoke, 3 great chances and a ridiculous unpunished handball from Toure. #scfc

08/03/2017
Rob Doolan@ChiefDelilah

Pieters' best game for months up to now.

08/03/2017
Will@IamWillSCFC

I've questioned Mark Hughes and his tactics numerous times this season. That was excellent. Tactically spot on, nullifying Fraudiola

---

08/03/2017
Espleypotter@Marcespley

Can that put to bed the notion that Stoke don't train with defensive formation and tactics under Hughes.

08/03/2017
Danny Bowers@dannybowers10

@oatcakescfc Fantastic performance. Showed grit in defence and a danger in attack. Shawcross was immense today, proved me wrong.

08/03/2017
Clive Bickley@Bickers1952

Cameron makes such a difference for us and he's been a big miss since October. Need to keep going now and finish on a high.

08/03/2017
BadManners@BringontheHippo

@virginmedia I've lost Comedy Central today. Was watching it last night. Any reason for this?

09/03/2017
Will@IamWillSCFC

Performances like last night are the reason I've been so critical of Ryan this season. That's what he's capable of. Truly magnificent!

09/03/2017
David Lee@stoke_city_pub

Mark Hughes has 2 years left on his #scfc contract. Should he be offered an extension? 35% an xtra 2 yrs, 11% an xtra year, 42% leave as is, 12% he won't last 2 yrs

09/03/2017
Dorset potter@cain_rosscain

guess what, we're not here to make you look good. if you can't break down a decent defence that is entirely your problem 😄

09/03/2017
Martin Smith@SolarSmudge

Still buzzing about Stoke's result last night. A real team performance and a thoroughly deserved draw. Outstanding!

18/03/2017   Stoke City (1) 1 Chelsea (1) 2

(The Champions-to-be are held up impressively...well, apart from Lee Grant misjudging a free-kick at his near post (0-1) and Pieters misjudging at the death (1-2). Walters' penalty is Stoke's only shot on target, but Chelsea celebrate at the end like they've won the league already.)

Premier League position: 9th

Order on MotD: 2nd out of 7

18/03/2017
Rob Doolan@ChiefDelilah

Does anything sap the will to watch a televised game than the words "and with me is Martin Keown"?

18/03/2017
Trouserdog@TrouserdogSCFC

Just realised we'll be cheering Arsenal on in the lunchtime game. That's going to feel...filthy.

17/03/2017
David Lee@stoke_city_pub

Stoke have only won 4 times in London in a single season ONCE! 2009/10

18/03/2017
Martin Smith@SolarSmudge

Chelsea, the football equivalent of the scummy family who win the lottery - all the money in the world but not one ounce of class!

18/03/2017
DUCK MAGAZINE@DUCKmagstoke

Fantastic following of 2800 from Chelsea. Which means there are 2800 fewer people shopping in Reading today.

18/03/2017
Rob Doolan@ChiefDelilah

Eddie Grant would've saved that.

18/03/2017
David Cowlishaw@davidcowlishaw

Can't be too upset with that. Gave them a game, the atmosphere was back and it felt like 'Stoke' again.

18/03/2017
Rob Doolan@ChiefDelilah

The Shaqiri situation is perplexing. The Imbula one really isn't.

18/03/2017
The Oatcake Fanzine@oatcakescfc

Great effort from Stoke. Pity our left back decided to defend like a League 2 plodder to gift Chelsea the points.

18/03/2017
Neil Finney@NeilFinney

That performance from Diego Costa. A grown man. Embarrassing.

18/03/2017
David Cowlishaw@davidcowlishaw

As hard working as we were today, we were shocking on the ball. Game crying out for Aff or that lad we signed from Porto...Imbolo? Imbrella?

18/03/2017
DUCK MAGAZINE@DUCKmagstoke

Feels like a defeat, that

18/03/2017
Dorset potter@cain_rosscain

Well done both teams that was a proper game with a proper atmosphere I paid for a seat but only used the edge of it. How it should be 👏👏👏

18/03/2017
Martin Smith@SolarSmudge

Going to positive today. That's three straight decent displays. Keep that going to the end of the season and we'll be fine! #stoke #scfc

18/03/2017
David Lee@stoke_city_pub

West Brom & Stoke City are 1 & 2 on #MOTD !?! What is the world coming to?! #scfc

20/03/2017
Trouserdog@TrouserdogSCFC

Quick tip for some fans re: Berahino. Being patient doesn't mean 'for 2 games'. Some of you would have written Steino off when he first came

25/03/2017
BadManners@BringontheHippo

Imbula. he has the attributes to be the next Vieira Just not showing it

25/03/2017
BadManners@BringontheHippo

I'd keep imbula & shaq. Bojan for me can go. Great player but lacks work rate and head drops to easy

26/03/2017
Espleypotter@Marcespley

Souttar: All the players respect Mark Hughes. Another notion quashed

27/03/2017
David Lee@stoke_city_pub

The brilliant #SCFC Harry Soutar on Mark Hughes: "The manager...he's so well respected down there. When he speaks, no-one else does."

01/04/2017   Leicester City (1) 2 Stoke City (0) 0

(Bloody Foxes! Bloody Robert Huth! Not the right time to play Leicester as they are suddenly back on the rails, but only two super-strikes by The Foxes is the real difference between these two Cities.)

Premier League position: 9th

Order on MotD: 5th out of 8

01/04/2017
David Cowlishaw@davidcowlishaw

Could be a vintage Hughesy 4er, this.

01/04/2017
HAIRY POTTER@cosnakickbo

King Power Stadium Asked for Plain Crisps They Said "We only have Ready Salted, Cheese & Onion and Smokey Bacon" 😂😂😂 @walkers_crisps

---

01/04/2017
Trouserdog@TrouserdogSCFC

Lucky not to be 2 or 3 down really. Walters has been abysmal. Hopefully Sparky will have given them all a bollocking.

01/04/2017
DUCK MAGAZINE@DUCKmagstoke

Let's see if Leicester camp on the edge of their own box and piss a two goal lead away KLAXON

01/04/2017
Rob Doolan@ChiefDelilah

Nice to see Huth and Shawcross trying to one-up each other in the 'acts of casual violence' stakes. Takes me back.

01/04/2017
Trouserdog@TrouserdogSCFC

Johnson and Pieters both paying tribute to Jonathan Woodgate's infamous full back appearance here.

01/04/2017
BadManners@BringontheHippo

As soon as I saw the midfield I knew. Whelan and Adam both need a three. Hughes sees them every day and should recognise this.

01/04/2017
Rob Doolan@ChiefDelilah

Beyond turgid from Stoke. Turns out Geoff Cameron was holding things together with masking tape. And that's a bleak place to be.

01/04/2017
HAIRY POTTER@cosnakickbo

PLAN B Take the Old Uns Off Bring the Old Uns On

01/04/2017
Rob Doolan@ChiefDelilah

Think I'm reluctantly at the stage where I'm ready for a change of manager.

01/04/2017
The Oatcake Fanzine@oatcakescfc

Usual deficiencies from Stoke. No pace, poor finishing and a lack of a plan. First murmurings against the manager as well today. Not good.

01/04/2017
Rob Doolan@ChiefDelilah

Utterly wretched. Side looks like an episode of Last of the Summer Wine. Old, tired and painfully unfunny.

01/04/2017
Clive Bickley@Bickers1952

Depressing! Needs to be said this season has been so poor. Want us to get safe and it to end now. Big decisions and clear out in the summer?

01/04/2017
David Lee@stoke_city_pub

Stoke City 52% possession away to Leicester - nil points. West Brom 25% possession away to Manchester United - one point...but last on MOTD.

01/04/2017
Dorset potter@cain_rosscain

Just forked out a grand for next season and w t f have we got to look forward to when a loose against Chelsea is the highlight of this one

01/04/2017
Rob Doolan@ChiefDelilah

Bournemouth have a team of suspiciously vague sounding names, like they're all part of the Witness Protection Programme.

03/04/2017
Dave@davematthews79

Turned over my Stoke calendar to April. It's the only place I'll be seeing Imbula, Bony or Given any time soon!

04/04/2017   Burnley (0) 1 Stoke City (0) 0

(Stoke have now played TWENTY mid-week Premier League away games...and lost 15 of them, winning only ONE (Fulham back in 1846 or summat). Burnley, usually so good at home, are poor, but Stoke just seem clueless to take advantage, particularly after the Clarets take the lead on the hour. But the game is more famous for Charlie Adam tripping over whilst taking a corner. You can't buy fame like that.)

Premier League position: 12th

Order on MotD: 10th out of 10

04/04/2017
DUCK MAGAZINE@DUCKmagstoke

This game will take some losing, but f*** me, if there's one team that can do it.....

04/04/2017
Chris Ault@Chrisa020985

Surely Bardsley a better option on the bench than Johnson?

04/04/2017
David Cowlishaw@davidcowlishaw

Charlie Adam, a man who's job it is to kick a football, fell over whilst attempting to kick a stationary football. He plays for my team.

04/04/2017
Trouserdog@TrouserdogSCFC

Completely bossed this game until they scored- now we're just hoofing it aimlessly. Wank.

04/04/2017
The Oatcake Fanzine@oatcakescfc

Same shit, different away day. Our final ball and finishing are an embarrassment for a team at this level at times. Thoroughly depressing.

04/04/2017
Will@IamWillSCFC

Diego Arismendi didn't die for this

04/04/2017
Martin Smith@SolarSmudge

The refusal of Stoke players to take a shot when they have a clear sight of goal is absolutely killing us! #scfc #stokecity

04/04/2017
Clive Bickley@Bickers1952

FFS why do we continue to be the charity team of the Prem when playing teams with a poor record. Burnley not won since January. Enough said.

04/04/2017
Will@IamWillSCFC

Did Shawcross cup his ears to the Stoke fans again tonight?

04/04/2017
David Lee@stoke_city_pub

After more defeats, poor performances, & after 31 games & only 34 points Stoke City sank into the bottom half of the league... #2012/13

04/04/2017
DUCK MAGAZINE@DUCKmagstoke

Fair play, we're quickly turning a meaningless end of season run of flip-flop games into a potential relegation battle. Takes some doing

04/04/2017
Will@IamWillSCFC

Would anyone grumble if we sacked Hughes tonight and had a caretaker manager until the Summer?

04/04/2017
Martin Smith@SolarSmudge

Lost to a team who had only one genuine goal attempt all night. That took some doing didn't it. I despair! #scfc #StokeCity

05/04/2017
David Cowlishaw@davidcowlishaw

I'm giving Hughes the next game. Not to get a result, but to demonstrate he knows how to manage this team. If not, then he's done for me.

05/04/2017
Neil Finney@NeilFinney

Not sure what was funnier Arnie shinning one out for a goal kick or Charlie's corner. #comedygold

05/04/2017
Will@IamWillSCFC

Another abject performance/defeat, local paper reporting supporters unrest, a dicking looming on Saturday, the end is nigh 👏 👏 👏 #hughesout

06/04/2017
Neil Finney@NeilFinney

Stoke 8 points off 8th as well as 8 points off 18th. #justsaying

08/04/2017   Stoke City (1) 1 Liverpool (0) 2

(The "Substitution" game. With Stoke leading from a first half Walters header (from Shaqiri's cross), the managers decide to make their just-after-the-hour substitutions. Sparky strangely swaps Walters, who just loves scoring against Liverpool, with...Glenn Whelan? Meanwhile, wily Klopp brings on Firmino and Courtinho. Five minutes later and it's 1-2 to Liverpool, and 4 defeats in a row for Stoke. Firmino's goal even wins MotD's Goal Of The Month. But surely this could have been avoided?)

Premier League position: 13th

Order on MotD: 3rd out of 7

08/04/2017
Trouserdog@TrouserdogSCFC

IMPORTANT FITNESS NEWS: I've managed to shake off a raging hangover and will be fit to attend today's game. Bet Sparky was sweating on that

---

08/04/2017
Neil Finney@NeilFinney

So Mr Dean, apart from the fact that he was on a yellow why didn't you book Klavan? Awaiting your reply.

08/04/2017
Will@IamWillSCFC

Huge question mark over our fitness levels. How many times this season have we been absolutely crap in a second half? It's unacceptable

---

08/04/2017
Dorset potter@cain_rosscain

Well done sparky inspired substitution

08/04/2017
The Oatcake Fanzine@oatcakescfc

A substitution as bad and as negative as any we've seen in the Premier League years. Utterly baffling. A big week ahead for Sparky. #StoLiv

08/04/2017
David Cowlishaw@davidcowlishaw

A game pissed up the wall

08/04/2017
Rob Doolan@ChiefDelilah

I like Hughes as a bloke & think overall he's done a really good job. But this has been going on for 14 months now. What's going to change?

08/04/2017
Rob Doolan@ChiefDelilah

Enjoyed the game and thought Stoke played fairly well overall, but yet again the manager's unfathomable substitution has cost us.

08/04/2017
Neil Finney@NeilFinney

Refereeing decisions and substitutions aside surely it's the same old problem - missing too many good chances. Goals needed.

08/04/2017
Will@IamWillSCFC

How Mark Hughes picks the players and formation for each game (Spoiler: Imbulas name is on the wall behind him)

08/04/2017
Espleypotter@Marcespley

Hull, Swansea, Wet spam and Bournemouth. We need at least 6 points from those 4 games

08/04/2017
Clive Bickley@Bickers1952

If the government gave out health warnings for supporting a football team SCFC would be way ahead.. I'm a wreck to date!

11/04/2017
Will@IamWillSCFC

Make no mistake, we are in a relegation battle. And for that reason alone, Hughes simply won't survive this Summer.

(Heavy weather and great goals. Arnie actually gets a brilliant early goal that ISN'T ruled out for a change. But after Hull equalise after the break, Mark Hughes makes another one of those crazy substitutions, taking off Adam and Berahino (logical) and bringing on the old guard of Crouch and Walters (seemingly illogical). This time it works, as they combine to make it 2-1. Shaqiri then scores a goal of the season screamer from 30 yards. But you can't please everyone.)

Premier League position: 11th

Order on MotD: 3rd out of 7

15/04/2017
Trouserdog@TrouserdogSCFC

Rumour has it that Peter Coates will be bringing his daughter Denise to today's game!

15/04/2017
DUCK MAGAZINE@DUCKmagstoke

Running out to Coldplay second half...... We need points docking

---

15/04/2017
David Cowlishaw@davidcowlishaw

I'm Hughes Out, but do think that double sub was unfairly booed. Adam was rightfully hauled off and it changed a failing system.

15/04/2017
Rob Doolan@ChiefDelilah

Nice to see three quality goals go in today. Credit to the manager, his changes this week cleaned up the mess he created with his stupid 3-4-3

15/04/2017
David Cowlishaw@davidcowlishaw

Not wanting to defend the manager too much, but I also think the 'relies on Pulis players' argument is a bit bogus.

15/04/2017
Rob Doolan@ChiefDelilah

Positives today: Better use of subs, Muniesa in midfield, Bruno, link play between Shaq and Arnie.

15/04/2017
Dorset potter@cain_rosscain

Ok sparky you got that right

16/04/2017
Terry Conroy@TerryConroy

You won't see 3 better goals in any one game this season.3rd,my fav. Arnies vision,JW's touch,Crouchies finish sublime.Poetry in motion.!

21/04/2017
David Lee@stoke_city_pub

Bony & Saido both 10 games for Stoke. Bony scored 2...Saido none. MH: "But Bony is not our player, & that's the difference" #scfc Stoke City

22/04/2017   Swansea City (1) 2 Stoke City (0) 0

(Swansea couldn't buy a win, as they approached this game after 6 defeats and a 0-0 home draw with hopeless Middlesbrough. Enter Stoke "Generous-to-a-fault" City. And just to help them out, Arnie blasts a penalty off towards the Bristol Channel. Swansea score their second 60 seconds later. However, unexpectedly, Jack Butland is back in goal! Well, somebody's happy then.)

Premier League position: 121h

Order on MotD: 2nd out of 4

22/04/2017
David Lee@stoke_city_pub

If Stoke City win on Saturday, they will have done-the-double over 4 clubs in the top flight for first time in 48 years!! #scfc #stokecity

---

22/04/2017
David Cowlishaw@davidcowlishaw

I challenge anyone to watch Llorente's goal and explain what Ryan Shawcross is doing.

22/04/2017
Neil Finney@NeilFinney

One highlight of Stokes game today... I didn't go and there's beer in the fridge.

22/04/2017
Neil Finney@NeilFinney

And that shocking penalty will be Hughes' fault no doubt. Hit the bloody target man.

22/04/2017
David Cowlishaw@davidcowlishaw

I mean it matters fuck all now, but we should be putting Saido on pens

22/04/2017
Neil Finney@NeilFinney

Shaking my head before he even took that. Jeeeze.

22/04/2017
Dorset potter@cain_rosscain

Our problem now is that we couldn't organise a come back if we found Elvis alive 😠😠

22/04/2017
Neil Finney@NeilFinney

On the beach Stoke?

22/04/2017
BadManners@BringontheHippo

Do we ever keep a winning side or formation? MH pisses around to much

22/04/2017
David Cowlishaw@davidcowlishaw

Tactical nerd point: Having a midfield is often considered a good thing for a Premier League football club

22/04/2017
Neil Finney@NeilFinney

Next Stoke away goal? I'm going for September.

22/04/2017
Espleypotter@Marcespley

Good thing is next week v West Ham I will be bringing my lucky mascot

22/04/2017
Clive Bickley@Bickers1952

The charity called SCFC rolls into town again. Swansea no win in 6, most goals against you just know what's going to happen!

22/04/2017
Dorset potter@cain_rosscain

Last week's result just papered over the massive cracks ,no threat, no identity no passion ,and hopefully no fucking manager

22/04/2017
Martin Smith@SolarSmudge

Just want this season to end. It's been one big disappointment and today summed it up. 596 minutes without an away goal!!! #scfc

23/04/2017
Trouserdog@TrouserdogSCFC

Hughes has got 4 games to work out how the fuck he's going to use Berahino for next seas Needs a plan- quickly.

27/04/2017
Rob Doolan@ChiefDelilah

I'm as frustrated with the manager as anyone, but I do find this insistence on martyring those he's frozen out as absolutely bizarre.

23/04/2017
The Oatcake Fanzine@oatcakescfc

Stoke City top flight wins at Anfield since 1894 - 0 Crystal Palace top flight wins at Anfield since 2014 - 3 #depressing

28/04/2017
Rob Doolan@ChiefDelilah

15 wins and 53 goals in our last 51 league games. Two-thirds of those wins against bottom six teams. Conceding 3 or more in 13 games.

28/04/2017
Rob Doolan@ChiefDelilah

If Hughes genuinely can't fathom why "for some reason" people perceive this as a disappointing season, we really are in trouble.

29/04/2017   **Stoke City 0 West Ham United 0**

(Sometimes it's hard to believe that the former United maverick and prolific goal-scorer Mark Hughes is Stoke's manager. Why can't he get his players to score goals? Instead, Jack Butland wins today's Man-Of-The-Match; and even The Oatcake magazine announce in disbelief that their Player Of The Season is defender Martins-Indi, who at the 11th hour overtakes Joe Allen who's lead the table all season! Where are the strikers? Go on, guess. Nowhere near the goal, that's for sure.)

Premier League position: 12th

Order on MotD: 5th out of 5

29/04/2017
David Cowlishaw@davidcowlishaw

Saido Berahino will score a goal today.

29/04/2017
DUCK MAGAZINE@DUCKmagstoke

Heads-up for Hammers: That big green thing in front of you, the thing you can actually see from your seat, is a football pitch.

29/04/2017
Dave@davematthews79

can't understand what Sobhi has done wrong! We were crying out for a bit of pace and creativity today but he doesn't feature

---

29/04/2017
David Cowlishaw@davidcowlishaw

We managed to create some half decent chances in spite of a terrible system. Hughes doesn't have a clue.

29/04/2017
Clive Bickley@Bickers1952

Highlight of the afternoon was the half time game. Some classy players in the red and white. Proud parents eh?

29/04/2017
The Oatcake Fanzine@oatcakescfc

Both keepers were in outstanding form, but our lack of creativity is killing us. How on earth has Ramadan been cast aside? #stowhu

29/04/2017
Trouserdog@TrouserdogSCFC

MH got the system right today- really should have seen Sobhi at some point though. Must have pissed in the manager's tea or something.

29/04/2017
Rob Doolan@ChiefDelilah

Have seen worse Stoke displays but it's all so desperately uninspired. Was fairly easy for West Ham to blot us out.

29/04/2017
Will@IamWillSCFC

Still think this season has been utter shite and can't wait to see the back of Hughes

29/04/2017
Danny Bowers@dannybowers10

What a boring and lacklustre performance. But as fans we expect too much apparently. Ramadan sat on the bench again.

30/04/2017
Rob Doolan@ChiefDelilah

Are people seriously fretting about Swansea catching us? Behave yourselves.

06/05/2017 Bournemouth (0) 2 Stoke City (1) 2

(After 10.5 hours, Stoke finally score away from home. Ok, it's an own-goal from a corner, but a goal is a goal. It all starts with Harry Arter's appalling diving challenge on Joe Allen, for which he only gets a yellow. The sickening slow-motion replays show that he should have been locked up and the key thrown away. It spurs Stoke into action, but Bournemouth keep equalising.)

Premier League position: 13th

Order on MotD: 7th out of 7

06/05/2017
David Lee@stoke_city_pub

Stoke City did double over Bournemouth last season. Bournemouth aim to do the same to Stoke this season... #scfc

---

06/05/2017
Neil Finney@NeilFinney

Shocking challenge from #Arter. We say it every week but if that was a Stoke player it would have been a red card and rightly so.

06/05/2017
David Cowlishaw@davidcowlishaw

"Stoke players surround the referee" It's literally just Shawcross taking the referee aside. Come on now.

06/05/2017
David Lee@stoke_city_pub

Best moment, Stoke City fans singing "We're winning away, you must be shit, we're winning away!" #scfc

---

06/05/2017
BadManners@BringontheHippo

About time diouf was given a go up front. Not saying much but he is the best all round striker we have

06/05/2017
Rob Doolan@ChiefDelilah

Better from Stoke. We look so much better with Diouf up front.

06/05/2017
Neil Finney@NeilFinney

Diouf scores. Bet he's on the bench next week.

06/05/2017
The Oatcake Fanzine@oatcakescfc

Chant of the Day at Bournemouth: "Norman Smurthwaite, he's one of our own".

06/05/2017
HAIRY POTTER@cosnakickbo

Get Ready for a Social Media Frenzy 1-1

06/05/2017
HAIRY POTTER@cosnakickbo

Alls Well Cancel The Meltdown 1-2 #BOUSTK Goarrrnnn You Potters 🍀🍀🍀🍀 Mame Biram Diouf #18 Goalllll

06/05/2017
Rob Doolan@ChiefDelilah

Should be noted that Arnie, even way off his game, has still essentially created both goals.

06/05/2017
Rob Doolan@ChiefDelilah

Another fucking gutless substitution.

06/05/2017
Will@IamWillSCFC

2 of the worst subs you'll ever see... unless you're a Stoke fan then you see this kind of shit every week #HughesOut

06/05/2017
Trouserdog@TrouserdogSCFC

Entertaining game, decent point, but fucking hell our finishing is absolutely dire. Should have had that game sewn up.

06/05/2017
Martin Smith@SolarSmudge

We had to work hard not to win that game. Terrible refereeing to be sure but we waste so many chances it's ridiculous. #scfc #stokecity

06/05/2017
Rob Doolan@ChiefDelilah

Suppose scoring away and a point isn't a terrible result, but we should've won and the manager's subs again killed our attacking threat dead

06/05/2017
The Oatcake Fanzine@oatcakescfc

Disappointing not to have won the game. We just can't kill teams off. Good to see two goals, but again what was that late sub all about?

06/05/2017
Rob Doolan@ChiefDelilah

If we end up finishing above West Brom I will be forced to pollute my trousers in amusement.

07/05/2017
Chris Ault@Chrisa020985

What do you guys think of Harry Arter's challenge on Joe Allen yesterday? He could've ended Allen's career with that #horrendous

06/05/2017
Next season's shirt designs

(Stoke's new strip for 2017-18 leaks out on to the web. You can't go wrong with red and white stripes, they say, but what about that blue away shirt…?)

06/05/2017
The Oatcake Fanzine@oatcakescfc

Congratulations to Macron on your French presidential election victory. That Stoke away top you've come up with is a mare though.

08/05/2017
Neil Finney@NeilFinney

For a second then I thought we really had launched that blue away kit.

06/05/2017
HAIRY POTTER@cosnakickbo

Bargain Workwear Will We Get Name Badges Hairy Potter Store Assistant #awayshirt

07/05/2017
Will@IamWillSCFC

Hardly slept following an awful nightmare. A shiny blue away shirt with a white collar, pink button and red and white horizontal stripes

08/05/2017
Neil Finney@NeilFinney

Go on Stoke, tell us there's stripes on the back of that home shirt.

08/05/2017
Neil Finney@NeilFinney

That Macron kit deal will save me a fortune.

13/05/2017   Stoke City (0) 1 Arsenal (1) 4

(Stoke have now only beaten teams below them, all of them in fact, and failed to beat any of the teams above them! This is reinforced as Arsenal make mincemeat of them in front of their own fans and the Sky cameras. Crouch scores brilliantly from a scorcher cross by Arnie, but slo-mo shows that it hit his hand not his head. But after a vote on social-media, the goal is still seen as brilliant coz it's against Arsenal. Gooners want Arsene Wenger to go, but Stoke fans wind them up, telling him they want him to stay! However, the lap of honour…I mean the lap of appreciation…is a little subdued.)

Premier League position: 14th

Order on MotD: 4th out of 7

13/05/2017
Will@IamWillSCFC

I'd accept this dog of a season if it culminates in us stopping the nonces reaching the top 4 today. I'm that fickle and bitter

---

13/05/2017
Espleypotter@Marcespley

Glen Johnson has completed 2 of his 10 passes. 20% pass completion Ffs. That 5 year old level

---

13/05/2017
Rob Doolan@ChiefDelilah

New drinking game: Drink every time the ball goes anywhere near Glen Johnson. Just to get through it.

13/05/2017
Espleypotter@Marcespley

Corbyn has more chance of winning the GE, than Stoke have of winning this.

14/05/2017
Neil Finney@NeilFinney

As a bare minimum fans 'expect' a fighting spirit from their team. Not evident for weeks.

13/05/2017
David Lee@stoke_city_pub

Sky commentator going on & on about Ramsey's leg is almost deliberately inflammatory. #scfc @SkySports

13/05/2017
BadManners@BringontheHippo

Don't forget. If we had bojan we'd be winning this 7-4

14/05/2017
Neil Finney@NeilFinney

Stayed for the end season player walk round. Some decent goals from the players kids to be fair.

13/05/2017
Espleypotter@Marcespley

Hope the fact only 5000 stayed for the lap of honour has give them something to think about

13/05/2017
Espleypotter@Marcespley

He needs to now bring in his own grit, but grit that can also be technical on the ball. 6 of those today need replacing

13/05/2017
The Oatcake Fanzine@oatcakescfc

No dressing that up. An abject and embarrassing performance. Massive changes are needed at this club or trouble awaits. #SCFC

13/05/2017
Danny Bowers@dannybowers10

@oatcakescfc Do I need to say anything? Get out Mark Hughes.

13/05/2017
Dorset potter@cain_rosscain

Mark seriously I don't know who you supported as a kid but how many times could you stomach them being thrashed 4 -1 in a season?

13/05/2017
Chris Ault@Chrisa020985

Horrendous, shit, dyer, boring, wank. There are no words for how poor that performance was and to be honest sums up our season.

14/05/2017
Clive Bickley@Bickers1952

Conceded 4 goals 7 times this season so of the 56 conceded in total 28 have been scored against us in 30! Any logic in this?

14/05/2017
Dorset potter@cain_rosscain

Just watched the lowlights on sky it's worse than I remember

15/05/2017
Neil Finney@NeilFinney

Poor run? Is that the Aug/Sept poor run, the Feb poor run or the April/May poor run?

14/05/2017
Rob Doolan@ChiefDelilah

The problem with the "it's only one bad season" argument is that it rather ignores the fact we only won 6 of our last 19 last season too.

13/05/2017
David Lee@stoke_city_pub

Two wins in last 12 games? Same as 2012-13, when the manager got sacked after Stoke's last game at...Southampton! History repeating?

13/05/2017
Will@IamWillSCFC

Absolute car crash of a season. If Mark Hughes had anything about him he'd resign tonight #HughesOut

13/05/2017
Espleypotter@Marcespley

Yes, a lot of the players Hughes has brought to the club have let him down

13/05/2017
Dave@davematthews79

I'd rather put bleach in my eyes than endure watching Stoke City again this season

13/05/2017
DUCK MAGAZINE@DUCKmagstoke

If you're not shitting your pants about next season you don't have any pants on.

14/05/2017
Rob Doolan@ChiefDelilah

My shortlist for Hughes replacements would be: Favre, Wagner, Silva, Schmidt, Jokanovic. Big no to: Mancini, Ranieri, Dyche, Pardew, Bruce.

16/05/2017
David Cowlishaw@davidcowlishaw

If we start next season badly (we will), we'll have to start again with a new manager with no time and transfer window to save us.

17/05/2017
DUCK MAGAZINE@DUCKmagstoke

Well done to Crouchy on winning the Top Goalscorer award. Hard luck to Own Goal though, very close, better luck next season.

20/05/2017
Danny Bowers @Dannybowers10

Only @stokecity would a player clean sweep the player of the year awards, only to be dropped while under-performing players play every week.

21/05/2017
Bad Manners @Bringonthehippo

Fuck sexy football. I want a game plan and not constant unnecessary team changes.

20/05/2017
Dorset Potter @cain_rosscain

We don't want sexy we want winning ,sexy can come later

20/05/2017
David Lee @Stoke_city_pub

Yes, a big moment in sporting history: Tony Pulis has finally finished in the top half of the Premier League!!

21/05/2017   **Southampton (0) 0 Stoke City (0) 1**

(Unbelievably, Stoke get a win on the last game of the season, putting them, as Mark Hughes observes, just 2 points off 8th spot. But a-miss-is-as-good-as-a-mile, and they actually finish 13th. Whereas Southampton get the converted 8th spot, and are crowned "champions of middle-Premier"...and are promptly booed off by their own supporters! Blimey, there's no pleasing some folk. It's Sparky 150th league win as a manager, Crouch's 50th Premier League headed goal (a record), a Stoke goalscorer has finally reached double figures, and it's Stoke's shortest season - only 41 games played in all - since 1906. But it doesn't go unnoticed that former manager Tony Pulis not only finishes above Stoke, but that his Albion snatch the kings-of-the-midlands trophy. Still, after being ignored by Match Of The Day for the whole season, at least now the BBC will give Stoke the coverage it deserves...?)

Premier League Position 13th.

Order on MotD: 10th out of 10.

21/05/2017
Neil Finney @NeilFinney

Stoke looking to secure last spot on #motd again this week.

21/05/2017
HAIRY POTTER @Cosnakickbo

CROUCHIEEEEEECCCEEEE 🍺 👍

21/05/2017
The Oatcake Magazine @Oatcakescfc

A good win to end a frustrating season. The table shows that we're not the only team to have had a poor season, but we do need to improve.

21/05/2017
DUCK MAGAZINE @DUCKmagstoke

Whelan, excellent today, especially when needed when we were on the back foot first half

21/05/2017
Neil Finney @NeilFinney

Not the best season but come on guys @petercrouch got his 100th Prem goal, did the robot and gave his shirt to a bloke in a snorkel.

21/05/2017
Will @IamWillscfc

Can we bring back Pink Panthers next season?

21/05/2017
DUCK MAGAZINE @DUCKmagstoke

Strange game, we were the better team but Butland the busier keeper

21/05/2017
Espleypotter @marcespley

Only 7 fewer shots this season compared to last

21/05/2017
DUCK MAGAZINE @DUCKmagstoke

Ace that the last thing football supporters will see on MOTD this season is Stoke winning away and a great mental

21/05/2017
Rob Doolan @ChiefDelilah

Now let us never speak of this season again.